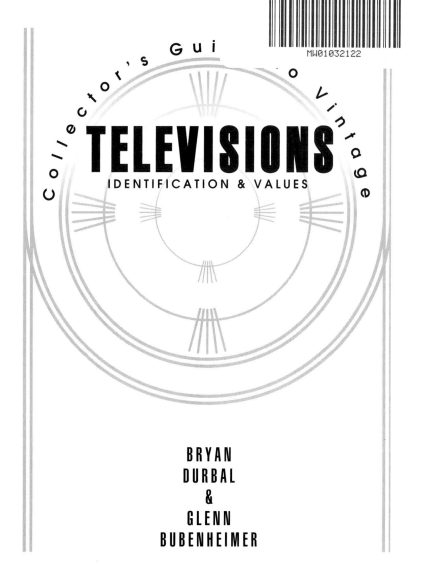

Collector's Guide to Vintage

TELEVISIONS

IDENTIFICATION & VALUES

BRYAN
DURBAL
&
GLENN
BUBENHEIMER

COLLECTOR BOOKS

A Division of Schroeder Publishing Co., Inc.

MW01032122

The current values in this book should be used only as a guide. They are not intended to set prices, which vary from one section of the country to another. Auction prices as well as dealer prices vary greatly and are affected by condition as well as demand. Neither the authors nor the publisher assumes responsibility for any losses that might be incurred as a result of consulting this guide.

Searching For A Publisher?

We are always looking for knowledgeable people considered to be experts within their fields. If you feel that there is a real need for a book on your collectible subject and have a large comprehensive collection, contact Collector Books.

Front cover: AMC (Aimee Wholesale Corp.) Console TV 120C, 12", mahogany wood, console, 1950, $40.00; Philco Predicta UG – 4710, 21", blond wood, console, two piece, screen on lond cord, "Penthouse," 1959, $350.00; Motorola 9VT1, 8", red mahogany, table top, chassis TS-18, 1949, $100.00.

Back cover: Philco Predicta UG – 4242M, 21", mahogany wood, table top, "Holiday," 1958, $200.00; Raytheon, 7DX22P, 7", cloth covered, portable, 1948, $125.00; Citizen, O6TA-OA, 2", gray plastic, hand held, LCD, transistor, 1987, $75.00.

Cover design by Beth Summers
Book design by Mary Ann Hudson

COLLECTOR BOOKS
P.O. Box 3009
Paducah, Kentucky 42002-3009

Copyright © 1999 by Bryan Durbal and Glenn Bubenheimer

All rights reserved. No part of this book may be reproduced, stored in any retrieval system, or transmitted in any form, or by any means including but not limited to electronic, mechanical, photocopy, recording, or otherwise, without the written consent of the authors and publisher.

CONTENTS

Contents

Contents

DEDICATION

This book is dedicated to all the wives and some husbands who put up with the time and mess of our collecting hobbies. God bless (help) them all!

You know you're a "diehard" radio/television collector when:

The mess and clutter of radio and television parts has taken over the house.

You say, to your wife or husband as you are working on your TV/Radio, "just one more minute and I'll be right there" ... and two hours go by.

You tell your wife/husband "It's only one more radio/television, I swear it will be the last one."

When gold, silver, and Catalin are precious commodities.

When you vacation in Rochester, Elgin, Lansing, Charlotte, etc...

A flashlight is needed to attend a swap meet.

You camp out at the mail box for the ARC to come.

ACKNOWLEDGMENTS

We would like to thank all the wonderful people who contributed information, facts, figures, and pictures to this publication. Without you this book would not have been possible! Craig Roberts for his information and pictures on projection television sets, Marty Bunis for his contribution of information and pictures of transistor television sets, not to mention all the helpful information on the publisher of this book. Thanks to all those who donated pictures, catalogs, and suggestions. We appreciate your encouragement and support! And finally to our wives and children for all the time sacrificed to make this book possible.

PREFACE

Welcome to the world of vintage television collecting. This guide was designed to help identify and estimate the value of post-war [1946 and later] televisions. Although television roots extend back to the late 1920s, this guide only references televisions of the post-war era. Pre-war televisions are of a greater historical significance, not to mention value and scarcity. Television collecting has gained popularity in the last five years especially with the **retro** collecting craze. How many times have you seen a vintage television [e.g. Philco Predicta] used in commercial advertisements? With the popularity boom of television collecting, what was once a cheap junk television is now a valuable eclectic piece of American pop culture.

Like radio collecting, television collectors have a variety of different models, styles, shapes, and sizes to pick from. You will find collectors that prefer only television sets with seven inch picture tubes, or others that collect only televisions with round picture tubes. Some televisions are valued for their historical significance. There are many milestone items such as Pilot model TV-37, the first television priced under $100.00, and early color televisions such as RCA model CT-100 circa 1955. Television/radio/phonograph combination sets, some large consoles, sets with rectangular picture tubes have a lower value due to their cumbersome size.

Unlike antique radios, vintage televisions do not have much appeal to the average radio collector, antique dealer, or eclectic person. This is due to the often costly restoration work it may take to rejuvenate a television to proper working order. Please take notice I say **restoration** and not **repair.** Restoring a television requires a complete replacement of all the electrolytic capacitors and any other questionable component. Repairing a set by replacing only one or two capacitors may be only a temporary fix. Many of the aforementioned individuals prefer a working television. Other than television collectors, there are not many people who want something that does not work.

I hope you find this book informative as well as enlightening. Please realize that there will be some inaccuracies with information listed. This guide was written expecting criticism. If you feel information listed is inaccurate, please inform us. We would like this publication to be as useful and accurate as possible. We hope you understand we cannot possibly please everyone with the prices listed. Although one may feel some of the prices may not be accurate, we have done our best to research this area. We invite your comments!

Thank you,

Bryan C. Durbal

Glenn Bubenheimer

CAUTION

Please read carefully.

Due to the nature of collecting, the prices reflect only the general opinion of the buyer and seller. It is in one's best interest to pay only what you feel an item is worth to you and you only! "What is one man's junk is another man's treasure" are words of wisdom to collect by. The prices in this guide are **only** the researched opinion of the author and only a researched opinion. The author assumes no responsibility for gains or losses due to this publication.

This book is designed to be used as a reference guide to identify and price vintage post-war televisions. The prices in this book are only a reference. The prices in this book were compiled from many different data sources. The price reflects the average market value of a television or a working transistor television in good condition, and only the model listed.

Non-working tube type
Good condition is defined as:
Complete with all tubes, correct knobs, and back cover.
Cabinet is not damaged, nice original finish.
Chassis is not rusty.
Chassis is correct, unmodified, and complete.
Good CRT [picture tube].
Having all accessories [i.e. antenna, handle, lid, etc.].

NOTE: Items or components that are missing, poorly refinished cabinets, or sets in poor condition can **dramatically** lower the value of the set. Prices should be adjusted accordingly.

DEFINITIONS

The following terms are used thoughout this guide:

AC – alternating current
AM – amplitude modulation
Color – color viewed picture
Console – floor model set
Consolette – small or miniature size floor model set
CRT – cathode ray tube or picture tube
DC – direct current
FM – frequency modulation
LCD – liquid crystal display
Leather/Leatherette – leather or simulated leather material covering the case
Portable – a set that may be transported to different locations; may have a built-in handle or carrying case
Projection – refers to the type of view generated from the CRT
Tabletop – refers to the tabletop sets

WARNING

If the condition of a television set is unknown, it should **not** be plugged in to check the operating condition. Severe injury or possible electrocution may result, as well as possible damage to the television set due to aging electronic components.

Because of the age of most early tube type televisions, most sets work poorly or do not work at all. The prices in this guide reflect a **non-working tube type** television or a working transistor type television. The following are also considered non-working: a poorly working set, picture and no sound, sound and no picture, etc. These symptoms often require a complete restoration of the set to make it function correctly. Restored tube type televisions that work properly often command a higher value due to the time, effort, and costly expense to restore them to working order.

Please take the above mentioned items into consideration when you buy or sell a television. Most collectors prefer a set that is unrestored, complete, and in good condition. Don't trouble yourself to restore a set to resell. Some sets that have little value may not be worth the effort to restore them. Good luck and happy collecting.

BLACK & WHITE TELEVISION SETS

Admiral

C2516, 24", wood, console, 1954, $25.00.

F2817, 27", wood, console, 1954, $25.00.

L2326, 21", wood, TV-radio/phono, console, 1952, $20.00.

T2316, 21", wood, 1952, $15.00.

T2317, 21", wood, 1952, $15.00.

4H15, 10", wood, TV-radio/phono, console, 1949, $20.00.

4H126, TV-radio/phono, console, 1949, $20.00.

8C11, 10", TV-radio/phono, console, 1948, $30.00.

12X12, 12", mahogany wood, tabletop, 1950, $25.00.

Black & White Television Sets

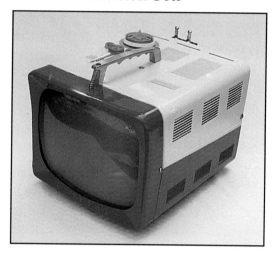

14YP3B, 12", metal, portable, 1956, $25.00.

14R12, 14", Bakelite, tabletop, 1951, $25.00.

16R12, 16", Bakelite, console, 1950, $50.00.

17T11, 7", brown or black Bakelite, tabletop, with "checker board" grille, 1948, $90.00.

17T12, 7", brown or black Bakelite, tabletop, with "checker board" grille, 1948, $90.00.

19A11, 7", black Bakelite, with "checker board" grille, 1948, $90.00.

19A11, 7", brown Bakelite, tabletop, with "checker board" grille, 1948, $90.00.

19A11, 7", brown or black Bakelite, with "Chinese" grille, 1948, $125.00.

19A11, 7", blond wood, tabletop, 1948, $100.00.

19A12, 7", brown or black Bakelite, tabletop, with "checker board" grille, 1948, $90.00.

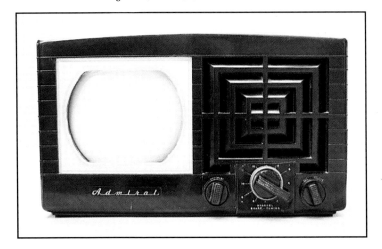

19A12, 7", black Bakelite, tabletop, with "Chinese" grille, 1948, $125.00.

Black & White Television Sets

19A15, 7", mahogany or blond wood, tabletop, 1949, $100.00.

20A1, 10", tabletop, 1949, $80.00.

20Y1, 10", tabletop, 1949, $80.00.

20B1, 12", wood, 1948, $80.00.

20T1, 14", Bakelite, console, 1949, $75.00.

20X112, 10", Bakelite, console, 1950, $125.00.

20Z1, 12", wood, 1948, $80.00.

21B1, 14", Bakelite, console, 1949, $75.00.

20X12, 10", Bakelite, console, four knobs, 1948, $175.00.

20X136, 12", mahogany wood, tabletop, 1949, $50.00.

22X12, 12", Bakelite, console, 1949, $85.00.

24A12, 12", Bakelite, console, 1949, $85.00.

20X11, 10", Bakelite, tabletop, four knobs, 1948, $80.00.

24R12, 14", Bakelite, console, 1950, $75.00.

26X46, 16", mahogany or walnut wood, rectangular tube, console, 1950, $20.00.

29X16, 19", blond wood, console, double doors, 1950, $35.00.

30A14, 10", wood, console, 1948, $100.00.

30B15, 10", wood, console, 1948, $100.00.

30F15A, 10", mahogany wood, TV-radio/phono, console, double doors, 1948, $40.00.

32X15, 12", walnut or mahogany wood, TV-radio/phono, console, 1950, $25.00.

32X27, 12", mahogany or blond wood, TV-radio/phono, console, 1950, $25.00.

32X35, 12", wood, TV-radio/phono, console, 1950, $25.00.

321F46, 20", wood, TV-radio/phono, "TELE-BAR" console, 1951, $160.00.

321K46, 20", wood, TV-radio/phono, "TELE-BAR" console, 1951, $160.00.

Aircastle

B76S-651M, 16", mahogany wood, tabletop, 1950, $75.00.

B76S-647M, 12", mahogany wood, tabletop, 1950, $100.00.

BS76-612M, 10", mahogany wood, tabletop, 1950, $115.00.

Air King

A-711, 12", wood, tabletop, 1950, $65.00.

A-712, 12", wood, tabletop, 1950, $65.00.

A-1000, 10", mahogany wood, tabletop, 1948, $120.00.

A-1001, 10", wood, tabletop, 1948, $120.00.

A-1001A, 10", wood, console, 1949, $110.00.

A-1016, 16", wood, console, 1949, $40.00.

A-2000, 10", wood, tabletop, 1949, $85.00.

A-2001, 12", wood, tabletop, 1949, $75.00.

A-2002, 12", wood, console, 1949, $75.00.

12C1, 12", wood, 1949, $75.00.

12T1, 12", wood, 1949, $75.00.

16C1, 16", wood, console, 1950, $30.00.

17C5-C, 17", mahogany wood, console, 1953, $40.00.

Black & White Television Sets
Airline (Montgomery Ward)

84HA-3002A, 7", wood, tabletop, 13 channel tuner, octal tubes, Hallicrafter with Airline logo, 1948, $145.00.

84HA-3002B, 7", wood, tabletop, 13 channel tuner, nine pin tubes, Hallicrafter with Airline logo, 1948, $125.00.

84GSE-3010A, mahogany wood, projection, console, double doors, 1948, $75.00.

84GSE-3011A, 7", black cloth covered, portable, Sentinel 400TV with Airline logo, 1948, $125.00.

84GSE-3011B, 7", gray cloth covered, portable, Sentinel 400TV with Airline logo, $125.00.

Airline (Montgomery Ward)

84HA-3010A, mahogany wood, projection, console, double doors, 1949, $75.00.

94BR-3004A, 10", mahogany wood, tabletop, 1949, $60.00.

94BR-3005A, 10", mahogany wood, console, 1949, $55.00.

94BR-3017A, 7", mahogany wood, tabletop, Raytheon 7DX21 with Airline logo, 1948, $125.00.

94GSE-3015A, 7", cloth covered, portable, with "Telephoto Control" button, 1948, $140.00.

Black & White Television Sets

94GSE-3018A, 7", mahogany wood, TV-radio/phono, tabletop, 45 rpm record player, 1949, $150.00.

94GSE-3025A, 16", mahogany wood, tabletop, 1949, $45.00.

94GSE-3033A, 16", mahogany wood, console, 1949, $40.00.

94WG-3006A, 10", blond wood, console, 1949, $70.00.

94WG-3009A, 10", mahogany wood, console, 1949, $60.00.

94WG3022A, 12", mahogany wood, tabletop, 1949, $50.00.

94WG-3029A, 12", blond wood, console, 1949, $60.00.

Airline (Montgomery Ward)

05GSE-3020A, 12", mahogany wood, tabletop, 1950, $35.00.

AMC (Aimcee Wholesale Corp.)

116T, 16", mahogany wood, tabletop, 1951, $65.00.

120C, 12", mahogany wood, console, 1950, $40.00.

Black & White Television Sets

Andrea

CO-VJ12-2, 12", wood, TV-radio, console, double doors, 1948, $90.00.

C-VJ12, 12", wood, console, 1948, $80.00.

C-VK12, 12", wood, console, 1948, $100.00.

C-VK15, 15", wood, TV-radio, console, 1948, $70.00.

CO-VK12, 12", wood, TV-radio/phono, console, 1948, $70.00.

CO-VK16, 16", wood, TV-radio, console, 1949, $75.00.

T-VJ12, 12", wood, TV-radio, tabletop, 1948, $125.00.

T-VK12, 12", wood, TV-radio, tabletop, 1948, $125.00.

Ansley

125, wood, projection, console, 1948, $70.00.

701, 10", wood, tabletop, "Beacon," 1948, $110.00.

702, 12", wood, tabletop, 1949, $70.00.

704, 12", blond wood, TV-radio/phono, console, "Belle-vue," 1948, $50.00.

705, 12", wood, TV-radio/phono, console, "Revere," 1949, $50.00.

Artone

**AR-23-TV-1, 10",
mahogany wood,
tabletop, 1948,
$140.00.**

Arvin

2120CM, 12", mahogany wood, console, chassis TE-289, 1949, $45.00.

2120CB, 12", blond wood, console, chassis TE-289, 1949, $55.00.

2121TM, 12", mahogany wood, tabletop, chassis TE-289, 1949, $65.00.

2122TM, 12", mahogany wood, tabletop, chassis TE-289, 1949, $65.00.

2123TM, 12", mahogany wood, tabletop, chassis TE-289, 1949, $65.00.

2124CCM, 12", mahogany wood, TV-radio/phono, console, double doors, chassis TE-289, 1949, $40.00.

2126CM, 12", mahogany wood, console, chassis TE-289, 1949, $40.00.

Black & White Television Sets

2160CB, 16", blond wood, console, chassis TE-290, 1949, $40.00.

2160CM, 16", mahogany wood, console, chassis TE-290, 1949, $40.00.

2161TM, 16", mahogany wood, tabletop, chassis TE-290, 1949, $35.00.

2162CCM, 16", mahogany wood, TV-radio/phono, console, double doors, chassis TE-290, 1949, $30.00.

2164CM, 16", mahogany wood, console, double doors, chassis TE-290, 1949, $40.00.

2164CM, 16", mahogany wood, TV-radio, console, double doors, chassis TE-290, 1950, $35.00.

3100TB, 10", blond wood, tabletop, chassis TE-272, 1949, $60.00.

3100TM, 10", mahogany wood, tabletop, chassis TE-272, 1949, $55.00.

3101CM, 10", mahogany wood, console, chassis TE-272, 1949, $50.00.

3120CB, 12", blond wood, console, chassis TE-272, 1949, $50.00.

3120CM, 12", mahogany wood, console, TE-272, 1949, $45.00.

3121TM, 12", mahogany wood, tabletop, chassis TE-272, 1949, $50.00.

3160CM, 16", mahogany wood, console, chassis TE-276, 1949, $40.00.

4080T, 8", metal, mahogany, limed oak, or willow green wood, photo-grain, tabletop, chassis TE-282, 1950, $110.00.

5204CM, 20", mahogany wood, console, chassis TE-300, 1950, $40.00.

5206CB, 20", blond wood, console, chassis TE-300, 1950, $50.00.

Black & White Television Sets

Atwater Television

12", mahogany wood, tabletop, 1949, $160.00.

Automatic

TV-707, 7", blond wood, tabletop, 1948, $200.00.

TV-709, 7", mahogany wood, tabletop, 1948, $200.00.

TV-710, 7", mahogany wood, console, 1948, $500.00.

TV-712, 7", blond wood, console, 1948, $500.00.

TV-P490, 7", leatherette, portable, with lid and built-in magnifier, 1948, $190.00.

TV-1049, 10", wood, tabletop, 1949, $80.00.

TV-1050, 10", wood, console, 1949, $60.00.

TV-1055, 10", wood, console, 1949, $60.00.

TV-1249, 12", wood, tabletop, 1949, $80.00.

TV-1250, 12", wood, console, 1949, $50.00.

TV-1649, 16", wood, tabletop, 1949, $50.00.

TV-1650, 16", wood, console, 1949, $40.00.

5006-T, 16", wood, tabletop, 1949, $50.00.

Base Television Corp.

150-D, 15", metal, tabletop, separate monitor with remote tuner, 1949, $85.00.

160-C, 16", mahogany wood, console, 12 channel tuner, 1949, $90.00.

160-TM, 16", mahogany wood, tabletop, 12 channel tuner, 1949, $90.00.

Black & White Television Sets

Belmont (see Raytheon-Belmont)

Bendix

235B1, 10", blond wood, tabletop, push-button tuner, double doors, 1949, $95.00.

235M1, 10", mahogany wood, tabletop, push-button tuner, double doors, 1949, $85.00.

325M8, 10", mahogany wood, TV-radio/phono, console, push-button tuner, 1949, $60.00.

2020, 12", mahogany wood, tabletop, 1950, $80.00.

2025, 12", mahogany wood, tabletop, 1950, $60.00.

2051, 16", mahogany wood, tabletop, 1950, $50.00.

3001, 10", mahogany wood, console, 1950, $55.00.

3030, 12", mahogany wood, console, 1950, $55.00.

3033, 12", mahogany wood, console, 1950, $50.00.

3051, 16", mahogany wood, console, 1950, $40.00.

6001, 16", mahogany wood, console, double doors, 1950, $25.00.

6002, 16", mahogany wood, console, 1950, $40.00.

6003, 16", mahogany wood, console, 1950, $40.00.

6100, 16", mahogany wood, TV-radio/phono, console, 1950, $25.00.

2001, 10", mahogany wood, tabletop, 1950, $110.00.

Black & White Television Sets
Bentley

100C, 4", gray plastic, portable, transistor, 1989, $60.00.

Capehart-Farnsworth

GV-260, 10", mahogany wood, tabletop, 1947, $225.00.

U-12-A, 10", mahogany wood, tabletop, 1949, $175.00.

2T216, 21", wood, tabletop, 1953, $20.00.

3T216, 21", wood, tabletop, 1953, $20.00.

8C215, 21", wood, console, 1953, $20.00.

22C215, 21", wood, console, three speakers in grille below, $15.00.

321M, 16", wood, tabletop, 1950, $30.00.

325F, 16", wood, console, double doors, 1950, $40.00.

661-P, 10", mahogany wood, tabletop, 1948, $150.00.

3001-B, 12", blond wood, tabletop, 1950, $65.00.

3001-M, 12", mahogany wood, tabletop, 1950, $50.00.

Capehart-Farnsworth

651-P, 10", mahogany
wood, tabletop, 1948,
$150.00.

4001-M, 12", mahogany wood, TV-radio/phono, console,
1950, $40.00.

Casio

**TV-21, 1½", LCD, transistor, hand
held, 1985, $45.00.**

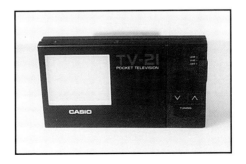

Black & White Television Sets

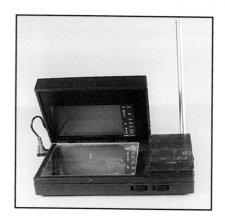

TV-30S, 2½", LCD, transistor, hand held, 1986, $55.00.

TV-100B, 1¾", LCD color display, hand held, 1988, $75.00.

TV-430, 1½", LCD color display, hand held, 1988, $35.00.

TV-470, 1½", LCD color display, hand held, 1988, $35.00.

TV-5100, 1⅘", plastic, Jeff Gordon, LCD, transistor, 1994, rare.

TV-5100, 1⅘", plastic, Dale Earnhart, LCD, transistor, 1994, rare.

CBS-Columbia

U22C05, 21", wood, console, with UHF tuner, 1955, $30.00.

U23C49, 21", wood, console, with UHF tuner, 1955, $30.00.

10FM, 10", wood, tabletop, rounded left top, Videodyne 10FM with CBS-Columbia logo, 1948, $170.00.

12FM, 12", wood, tabletop, rounded left top, Videodyne 12FM with CBS-Columbia logo, 1948, $160.00.

10TV, 10", wood, tabletop, rounded left top, Videodyne 10TV with CBS-Columbia logo, 1948, $170.00.

Black & White Television Sets

12TV, 12", wood, tabletop, rounded left top, Videodyne 12TV with CBS-Columbia logo, 1948, $160.00.

20C, 20", wood, console, 1950, $30.00.

20C3, 20", wood, console, double doors, 1951, $25.00.

20M, 20", metal, tabletop, 1950, $20.00.

20T, 20", wood, tabletop, 1950, $25.00.

22C05, 21", wood, console, 1955, $25.00.

22C07, 21", wood, console, 1955, $25.00.

22T09, 21", wood, tabletop, 1955, $25.00.

22T19, 21", wood, tabletop, 1955, $25.00.

23C49, 21", wood, console, 1955, $25.00.

23C59, 21", wood, console, double doors, 1955, $25.00.

Certified Radio Laboratories

47-71, 7", kit, no cabinet, supplied with six channel tuner, 1947, $180.00.

48-10, 10", kit, no cabinet, supplied with six channel tuner, 1948, $160.00.

49-10, 10", kit, no cabinet, supplied with five or 13 channel tuner, 1949, $150.00.

Citizen

06TA-0A, 2", gray plastic, LCD, hand held, transistor, 1987, $75.00.

Cleervue

Hollywood, 15", blond wood, console, pivot screen, long spindle legs, 1947, $400.00.

Regency, 15", mahogany wood, console, double doors, 1947, $100.00.

Coronado

FA-43-8965A, 7", wood, tabletop, Raytheon 7DX21 chassis, 1949, $120.00.

FA-43-8965B, 7", wood, tabletop, Raytheon 7DX21 chassis, 1949, $120.00.

TV43-8960, 10", wood, tabletop, 1949, $90.00.

94TV2-43-8970A, 10", mahogany wood, console, 1949, $70.00.

Black & White Television Sets

94TV2-43-8971A, 10", blond wood, console, 1949, $70.00.

94TV2-43-8972A, 12", mahogany wood, console, 1949, $50.00.

94TV2-43-8973A, 12", blond wood, console, 1949, 75.00.

94TV2-43-8985A, 10", mahogany wood, tabletop, 1949, $70.00.

94TV2-43-8986A, 10", blond wood, tabletop, 1949, $80.00.

94TV2-43-8987A, 12", mahogany wood, tabletop, 1949, $50.00.

94TV2-43-8993A, 10", mahogany wood, tabletop, 1949, $55.00.

94TV2-43-8994A, 10", blond wood, console, 1949, $80.00.

94TV2-43-8995A, 10", mahogany wood, console, 1949, $60.00.

94TV6-43-8953A, 12", mahogany wood, tabletop, 1950, $40.00.

Cromwell

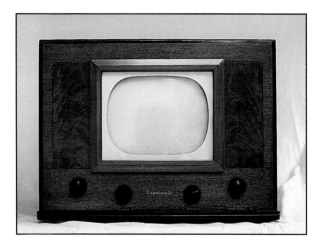

10", mahogany wood, tabletop, 1949, $150.00.

Crosley

EU-30, 30", wood, console, DuMont RA-119 with Crosley logo, 1952, $400.00.

F-17TOL, 17", wood, tabletop, 1954, $15.00.

F-21COB, 21", wood, console, 1954, $15.00.

F-21COL, 21", wood, console, 1954, $15.00.

F-27COB, 27", wood, console, 1954, $10.00.

G-17TO, 17", wood, tabletop, 1955, $25.00.

307-TA 10", wood, tabletop, RCA 630 chassis, 1948, $120.00.

348-CP, 10", wood, TV-radio/phono, console, "SWING-A-VIEW," 1948, $170.00.

9-403M, 10", mahogany wood, tabletop, Dumont continuous tuner, 1949, $75.00.

9-407, 12", mahogany wood, tabletop, 1949, Dumont continuous, tuner, $75.00.

9-409M, 12", mahogany wood, console, double doors, 1949, $50.00.

9-414, 10", wood, console, double doors, 1949, $75.00.

9-419M, 12", mahogany wood, tabletop, 1949, $100.00.

9-420M, 10", mahogany wood, console, 1949, $75.00.

9-422M, 16", mahogany wood, console, 1949, $35.00.

9-423M, 10", mahogany wood, TV-radio/phono, console, double doors, 1949, $55.00.

9-424B, 10", blond wood, console, 1949, $115.00.

9-425, 7", leatherette, portable, lid with handle, 1949, $140.00.

Black & White Television Sets

10-401, 10", Bakelite, tabletop, large white mask, 1950, $85.00.

10-414, 16", wood, console, double doors, 1949, $75.00.

10-416, 16", wood, console, 1949, $75.00.

10-419MU, 12", mahogany wood, console, 1950, $30.00.

10-420, 12", wood, console, 1950, $70.00.

10-428, 14", wood, tabletop, 1950, $40.00.

10-429, 16", wood, console, 1950, $25.00.

11-443, 19", mahogany wood, round tube, console, 1950, $65.00.

11-444, 17", mahogany wood, rectangle tube, TV-radio/phono, console, double doors, 1950, $25.00.

11-445, 16", mahogany wood, rectangle tube, console, 1950, $25.00.

11-446, 16", mahogany wood, round tube, console, 1950, $55.00.

11-447, 16", mahogany wood, rectangle tube, console, curved double doors, 1950, $35.00.

11-453, 17", mahogany wood, rectangle tube, console, 1950, $30.00.

11-454, 19", mahogany wood, round tube, console, double doors, 1950, $35.00.

11-458, 19", mahogany wood, round tube, console, double doors, 1950, $35.00.

11-459, 16", mahogany wood, rectangle tube, console, tall wooden legs, 1950, $45.00.

11-460, 17", mahogany wood, rectangle tube, console, double doors, 1950, $30.00.

11-465, 16", walnut wood, rectangle tube, console, 1950, $30.00.

11-466, 16", mahogany wood, round tube, console, 1950, $45.00.

11-472, 17", blond wood, rectangle tube, console, tall wooden legs, 1950, $60.00.

11-474, 17", mahogany wood, rectangle tube, TV-radio/phono, console, double doors, 1950, $35.00.

11-475, 16", blond wood, rectangle tube, console, 1950, $45.00.

11-476, 16", blond wood, round tube, console, 1950, $60.00.

11-477, 16", blond wood, rectangle tube, console, curved double doors, 1950, $50.00.

Black & White Television Sets

Crown

CVT-12, 5", transistor, TV/radio, portable, AC/DC, 1968, $45.00.

Delco

TV-71, 7", wood, tabletop, Hallicrafters with Delco name, uses Loctal base tubes, 1948, $175.00.

TV-71A, 7", wood, tabletop, Hallicrafters with Delco name, uses nine pin miniature tubes, 1948, $165.00.

TV-101, 10", walnut wood, tabletop, 1949, $90.00.

TV-102, 10", mahogany wood, tabletop, 1949, $90.00.

TV-121, 12", blond wood, console, 1949, $65.00.

TV-122, 12", mahogany wood, console, 1949, $55.00.

TV-160, 16", mahogany wood console, double doors, 1949, $40.00.

TV-201, mahogany wood, projection, console, double doors, 1949, $100.00.

DeWald

BT-100, 10", mahogany wood, tabletop, 1948, $100.00.

CT-101, 16", wood, console, 1949, $40.00.

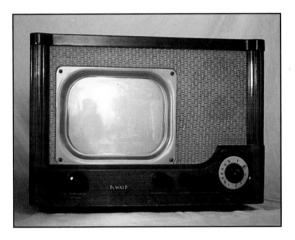

CT-102, 10", mahogany wood, tabletop, 1949, $80.00.

CT-103, 10", wood, console, 1949, $80.00.

CT-104, 10", wood, tabletop, 1949, $100.00.

DT-102, 10", wood, tabletop, 1949, $100.00.

DT-120, 12", wood, tabletop, 1949, $70.00.

DT-160, 16", wood, tabletop, 1950, $40.00.

DT-190, 19", wood, console, 1950, $25.00.

ET-140, 14", wood, tabletop, 1950, $25.00.

ET-171, 17", TV-radio/phono, 1951, $20.00.

DuMont

RA-101, 20", rack-mount [no cabinet], "Custom," 1947, $60.00.

RA-101, 15", blond wood, TV-radio/phono, console, double doors, "Devonshire," 1947, $280.00.

RA-101, 20", blond wood, TV-radio/phono, console, "Hamshire," 1947, $500.00.

RA-101, 15", natural wood, TV-radio/phono, console, double doors, "Plymouth," 1947, $60.00.

RA-101, 15", walnut wood, TV-radio/phono, console, double doors, "Revere," 1947, $60.00.

RA-101, 15", mahogany wood, TV-radio/phono, console, double doors, "Sherwood," 1947, $90.00.

RA-101, 20", dark mahogany wood, TV-radio/phono, console, "Westminster," 1947, $75.00.

RA-102, 15", mahogany wood, tabletop, "Club," 1947, $200.00.

RA-102, 12", mahogany-maple wood, console, "Clifton," 1947, $600.00.

RA102-B1, 12", mahogany-maple wood, console, "Clifton," 1947, $500.00.

RA-103, 12", maple wood, TV-radio, tabletop, trapezoid shape, "Chatham," 1947, $150.00.

RA103, 12", maple wood, TV-radio/phono, console, double doors, "Savoy," 1947, $80.00.

RA-103D, 12", mahogany wood, TV-radio, tabletop, "Stratford," 1947, $105.00.

RA-105, 15", mahogany wood, TV-radio/radio, console, "Colony," 1949, $50.00.

RA-105, 15", mahogany wood, TV-FM radio, tabletop, "Stratford," 1949, $75.00.

RA-105, 15", mahogany wood TV-FM radio, console, "Westbury," 1949, $60.00.

RA-105, 15", mahogany wood, "TV-FM radio, console, "Whitehall," 1949, $60.00.

RA-106, 20", mahogany wood, tabletop, "Club 20," 1949, $75.00.

RA-109-A1, 19", mahogany wood, TV-radio, console, "Winslow," 1950, $55.00.

Black & White Television Sets

RA-103D-3, 12", blond wood, TV-radio, console, "Savoy," 1947, $100.00.

RA-109-A2, 19", mahogany wood, TV-radio, console, double doors, "Hanover," 1950, $50.00.

RA-109-A3, 19", mahogany wood, TV-radio/phono, console, double doors, "Sherbrooke," 1950, $45.00.

RA-109-A5, 19", blond wood, TV-radio, console, "Winslow," 1950, $85.00.

RA-109-A6, 19", blond wood, TV-radio, console, double doors, "Hanover," 1950, $70.00.

RA-109-A7, 19", blond wood, TV-radio/phono, console, double doors, "Sherbrooke," 1950, $50.00.

RA-111-A1, 12", mahogany wood, tabletop, "Putnam," 1950, $75.00.

RA-111-A2, 12", mahogany wood, console, "Guilford," 1950, $75.00.

RA-111-A4, 12", blond wood, tabletop, "Putnam," 1950, $85.00.

RA-111-A5, 12", blond wood, console, "Guilford," 1950, $80.00.

RA-112, 15", mahogany wood, TV-radio, console, 1950, $65.00.

RA-119, 30", mahogany wood, console, double doors, "Royal Sovereign," 1952, $400.00.

Electro-Technical Industries

7-A, 7", kit TV, no cabinet, chassis and CRT are separate, 13 channel tuner, 1948, $150.00.

7-B, 7", kit TV, no cabinet, chassis and CRT are separate, 13 channel tuner, 1948, $150.00.

7-B, 7", kit TV with walnut cabinet, tabletop, 13 channel tuner, "Telekit," 1948, $200.00.

8B, 8", kit TV with walnut cabinet, tabletop, 12 channel tuner, "Telekit," 1949, $160.00.

Black & White Television Sets

10-A, 10", kit TV, no cabinet, chassis and CRT are separate, 13 channel tuner, 1948, $125.00.

10-B, 10", kit TV with walnut cabinet, 13 channel tuner, "Telekit," 1948, $180.00.

12B, 12", kit TV with walnut cabinet, tabletop, 12 channel tuner, "Telekit," 1949, $150.00.

Emerson

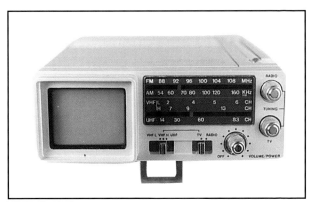

VR22, 2", gray plastic, transistor, TV/radio, portable, 1989, $50.00.

527, 10", maple wood, console, slanted front, 1948, $400.00.

585, 10", wood, TV-radio/phono, console, double doors, 1948, $60.00.

606, 10", wood, console, 1948, $80.00.

608, 16", wood, console, lid lift to swing out picture tube, 1949, $175.00.

609, wood, projection, console, "Protelgram," 1949, $125.00.

545, 10", walnut wood, tabletop, 1947, $160.00.

571, 10", walnut wood, tabletop, 1948, $110.00.

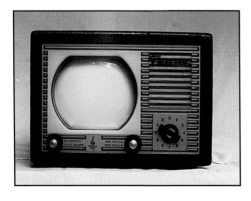

600, 7", leatherette, portable, gold reverse painted bezel, handle on side, 1949, $140.00.

610, 7", walnut wood, tabletop, gold reverse painted bezel, 1949, $150.00.

611, 10", wood, tabletop, reverse paint glass screen, 1948, $85.00.

614, 10", black Bakelite, tabletop, 1950, $80.00.

618, 12", TV-radio/phono, console, double doors, 1948, $50.00.

619, 10", wood, console, 1948, $75.00.

621, 10", wood, tabletop, 1948, $85.00.

622, 10", wood, TV-radio/phono, console, 1948, $70.00.

624, 10", mahogany wood, tabletop, 1948, $120.00.

626, 16", mahogany wood, console, 1949, $70.00.

628, 10", mahogany wood, TV-radio, tabletop, vertical slide-rule tuners, 1948, $100.00.

629C, 16", mahogany wood, console, 1950, $65.00.

630, 12", mahogany wood, TV-radio/phono, console, double doors, 1948, $65.00.

631, 16", mahogany wood, tabletop, 1950, $70.00.

632, 16", mahogany wood, TV-radio/phono, console, double doors, 1950, $50.00.

633, 16", mahogany wood, console, double doors, 1950, $60.00.

637, 10", mahogany wood, tabletop, 1948, $80.00.

638, 10", wood, console, 1948, $80.00.

639, 7", wood, tabletop, reverse gold painted bezel, 1949, $120.00.

644, 12", wood, tabletop, 1949, $75.00.

647, 12", wood, console, 1949, $70.00.

648, 10", Bakelite, tabletop, 1949, $75.00.

649, wood, projection, console, 1949, $100.00.

650, 12", mahogany wood, tabletop, 1949, $70.00.

Black & White Television Sets

651, 16", mahogany wood, tabletop, 1949, $45.00.

654, 12", mahogany wood, console, 1949, $50.00.

662, 14", Bakelite, tabletop, 1950, $25.00.

663, 14", mahogany wood, tabletop, 1950, $40.00.

666, 16", wood, TV-radio/phono, console, 1950, $20.00.

669, 19", wood, console, double doors, 1950, $25.00.

686, 17", wood, console, 1952, $25.00.

687, 17", wood, console, double doors, 1952, $25.00.

692, 20", wood, console, 1952, $15.00.

693, 20", wood, console, double doors, 1952, $15.00.

694, 20", wood, console, 1952, $15.00.

696, 17", wood, tabletop, 1952, $25.00.

697, 20", wood, console, long wood legs, on swivel stand, 1952, $30.00.

699, 17", wood, TV-radio/phono, console, 1952, $20.00.

1030, 14", leatherette, portable, 1955, $10.00.

1032, 14", leatherette, portable, 1955, $10.00.

1104, 21", wood, tabletop, 1955, $15.00.

1106, 21", wood, tabletop, 1955, $15.00.

Emerson

1444, 21", wood, TV-radio/phono, console, 1959, $20.00.

1472, 17", leatherette, portable, 1959, $20.00.

1504, 17", metal, portable, 1959, $35.00.

Empire State (see Western Television)

Epsey

Training kit, 3", green CRT, chassis only, seven knobs, no cabinet, 1947, $375.00.

Fada

R-1050, 16", wood, tabletop, 1950, $35.00.

S-1050, 12", wood, tabletop, 1949, $40.00.

S-1030, 12", mahogany wood, tabletop, 1950, $40.00.

S20C10, 20", mahogany wood, console, 1951, $25.00.

TV-30, 10", mahogany wood, tabletop, 1947, $150.00.

880, wood, projection, console, 1948, $70.00.

895, 12", wood, TV-radio/phono, console, double doors, 13 channel tuner, 1948, $60.00.

899, 10", wood, tabletop, 13 channel tuner, 1948, $130.00.

925, 16", wood, tabletop, 13 channel tuner, 1948, $70.00.

Black & White Television Sets

S-1070, 12", mahogany wood, tabletop, 1950, $40.00.

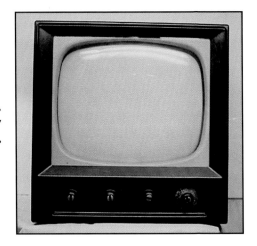

799, 10", wood, tabletop, with glass screen cover, 13 channel tuner, 1947, $150.00.

930, 12", wood, tabletop, 13 channel tuner, 1948, $90.00.

940, 12", wood, console, 13 channel tuner, 1948, $75.00.

965, 16", wood, console, 13 channel tuner, 1948, $60.00.

Farnsworth (see Capehart-Farnsworth)

Firestone

13-G-3, 7", mahogany wood, tabletop, 1948, $125.00.

13-G-4, 10", mahogany wood, tabletop, 1948, $65.00.

13-G-5, 10", mahogany wood, console, 1948, $60.00.

13-G-33, 7", leatherette, tabletop, built-in antenna, 1948, $110.00.

Black & White Television Sets

13-G-117, 17", mahogany wood, console, "Delmore," 1953, $25.00.

13-G-118, 21", mahogany wood, console, "Empire," 1953, $25.00.

13-G-124, 20", metal, tabletop, "Dawson," 1953, $20.00.

13-G-125, 17", metal, tabletop, "Colby," 1953, $30.00.

Freed Eisemann

54, 16", mahogany wood, console, chassis 1620C, 1949, $55.00.

55, 16", mahogany wood, console, chassis 1620C, 1949, $60.00.

56, 16", mahogany wood, console, chassis 1620C, 1949, $60.00.

77, 16", mahogany wood, tabletop, 1949, $80.00.

Gamble-Skogmo (see Coronado)

Garod

10TZ21, 10", blond wood, TV-radio, tabletop, "Malibu," 1949, $180.00.

10TZ22, 10", mahogany wood, TV-radio, console, "Monticello," 1949, $120.00.

10TZ23, 10", blond wood, TV-radio, console, "Catalina," $140.00.

10TZ20, 10", mahogany wood, TV-radio, table-top, "Amabassador," 1949, $170.00.

12TZ20, 12", mahogany wood, TV-radio, tabletop, "Belvidere," 1949, $150.00.

12TZ21, 12", blond wood, TV-radio, tabletop, "Claridge," 1949, $160.00.

12TZ22, 12", mahogany wood, TV-radio, console, "Coronet," $100.00.

12TZ23, 12", blond wood, TV-radio, console, "Carlton," $120.00.

15TZ24, 15", mahogany wood, TV-radio, tabletop, 1949, $130.00.

15TZ25, 15", blond wood, TV-radio, tabletop, 1949, $140.00.

15TZ26, 15", mahogany wood, TV-radio, console, 1949, $85.00.

Black & White Television Sets

15TZ27, 15", blond wood, TV-radio, console, 1949, $100.00.

900TV, 10", mahogany wood, tabletop, 13 channel tuner, 1948, $180.00.

910TV, 10", blond wood, tabletop, 13 channel tuner, 1948, $190.00.

920TV, 10", mahogany wood, TV-radio, tabletop, 13 channel tuner, 1948, $135.00.

921TVP, 10", mahogany wood, TV-radio/phono, console, double doors, 1948, $75.00.

930TV, 10", wood, TV-radio, tabletop, 13 channel tuner, 1948, $150.00.

1000TV, 12", wood, TV-radio, tabletop, 13 channel tuner, 1948, $150.00.

1000TVP, 12", mahogany wood, TV-radio/phono, console, double doors, 1948, $75.00.

1020TV, 12", wood, TV-radio, tabletop, 13 channel tuner, 1948, $115.00.

1021TVP, 12", mahogany wood, TV-radio/phono, console, double doors, 1948, $90.00.

1030TV, 12", blond wood, TV-radio, tabletop, 13 channel tuner, 1948, $140.00.

1043G, 10", blond wood, tabletop, 1949, $80.00.

1042G, 10", mahogany wood, tabletop, 1949, $70.00.

1200TVP, 10", mahogany wood, TV-radio/phono, console, double doors, 1948, $75.00.

1244G, 12", mahogany wood, tabletop, 1949, $60.00.

1245G, 12", blond wood, tabletop, 1949, $65.00.

1546G, 16", mahogany wood, tabletop, 1949, $45.00.

1547G, 16", blond wood, tabletop, 1949, $50.00.

1548G, 16", mahogany wood, console, 1949, $45.00.

1549G, 16", blond wood, console, 1949, $50.00.

1672, 16", mahogany wood, console, 1950, $25.00.

1673, 16", blond wood, console, 1950, $35.00.

Black & White Television Sets

1974, 19", mahogany wood, console, 1950, $20.00.

1975, 19", wood, console, 1950, $20.00.

3912, 12", wood, TV-radio/phono, console, 13 channel push-button tuner, 1947, $90.00.

3915, 12", wood, TV-radio/phono, console, 13 channel push-button tuner, double doors, 1947, $85.00.

General Electric

ASF-1703-GR, 9", trapezoid shaped, tabletop, transistor, 1984, $25.00.

9T001, 10", metal, tabletop, 1956, $25.00.

10C101, 10", mahogany wood, console, 1949, $35.00.

10C102, 10", blond wood, console, 1949, $35.00.

10T1, 10", Bakelite, tabletop, 1949, $125.00.

10T4, 10", mahogany wood, tabletop, 1949, $65.00.

10T5, 10", blond wood, tabletop, 1949, $65.00.

10T6, 10", Bakelite, tabletop, 1949, $125.00.

12C101, 12", mahogany wood, console, 1949, $50.00.

12C102, 12", blond wood, console, 1949, $55.00.

12C105, 12", walnut wood, console, 1949, $45.00.

12C107, 12", mahogany wood, console, 1949, $50.00.

12C108, 12", blond wood, console, 1949, $50.00.

12C109, 12", mahogany wood, console, double doors, 1949, $45.00.

12K1, 12", mahogany wood, TV-radio/phono, console, double doors, 1949, $35.00.

12T1, 12", wood, tabletop, 1949, $20.00.

Black & White Television Sets

12T3, 12", mahogany wood, tabletop, 1949, $75.00.

12T4, 12", blond wood, tabletop, 1949, $90.00.

12T7, 12", mahogany wood, tabletop, 1949, $60.00.

14C102, 14", mahogany wood, console, 1950, $20.00.

14C103, 14", blond wood, console, 1950, $20.00.

14T2, 14", mahogany wood, tabletop, 1950, $25.00.

14T3, 14", blond wood, tabletop, 1950, $25.00.

16C103, 16", mahogany wood, console, 1951, $35.00.

16C104, 16", blond wood, console, 1951, $40.00.

16C110, 16", mahogany wood, console, 1951, $35.00.

16C111, 16", blond wood, console, 1951, $40.00.

16C113, 16", mahogany wood, console, 1951, $30.00.

16C115, 16", mahogany wood, console, double doors, 1951, $30.00.

16C116, 16", mahogany wood, console, double doors, 1951, $30.00.

16K1, 16", mahogany wood, TV-radio/phono, console, double doors, 1950, $30.00.

16K2, 16", blond wood, TV-radio/phono, console, double doors, 1950, $35.00.

16T1, 16", mahogany wood, tabletop, 1951, $25.00.

16T2, 16", blond wood, tabletop, 1951, $30.00.

16T3, 16", mahogany wood, tabletop, 1951, $25.00.

16T4, 16", blond wood, tabletop, 1951, $30.00.

16T5, 16", mahogany wood, rectangular tube, tabletop, 1950, $25.00.

16C103, 16", mahogany wood, rectangular tube, console, 1950, $25.00.

17C101, 17", mahogany wood, rectangular tube, console, double doors, 1950, $25.00.

17C102, 17", blond wood, rectangular tube, console, double doors, 1950, $35.00.

Black & White Television Sets

17C103, 17", mahogany wood, console, 1950, $25.00.

17C104, 17", blond wood, console, 1950, $30.00.

17C105, 17", mahogany wood, console, 1950, $25.00.

17C107, 17", mahogany wood, console, double doors, 1950, $30.00.

17C108, 17", blond wood, console, double doors, 1950, $35.00.

17C109, 17", mahogany wood, console, double doors, 1950, $30.00.

17C110, 17", mahogany wood, console, double doors, 1950, $30.00.

17C111, 17", blond wood, console, double doors, 1950, $35.00.

17C112, 17", mahogany wood, console, 1950, $25.00.

17C113, 17", blond wood, console, short wooden legs, 1950, $40.00.

17C114, 17", mahogany wood, console, double doors, 1950, $30.00.

17C115, 17", blond wood, console, double doors, 1950, $35.00.

17C117, 17", mahogany wood, console, 1950, $25.00.

17C120, 17", mahogany wood, console, double doors, 1950, $35.00.

17T1, 17", mahogany wood, tabletop, 1950, $25.00.

17T2, 17", mahogany wood, tabletop, 1950, $25.00.

17T3, 17", blond wood, tabletop, 1950, $35.00.

17T5, 17", mahogany wood, tabletop, 1950, $35.00.

17T6, 17", blond wood, tabletop, 1950, $40.00.

17T7, 17", mahogany wood, tabletop, 1950, $30.00.

19C101, 19", mahogany wood, round tube, console, double doors, 1950, $55.00.

20C150, 20", mahogany wood, rectangular tube, console, double doors, 1951, $25.00.

20C151, 20", blond wood, rectangular tube, console, double doors, 1951, $30.00.

24C101, 24", mahogany wood, round tube, console, double doors, 1950, $70.00.

800, 10", Bakelite, tabletop, 1949, $125.00.

Black & White Television Sets

801, 10", mahogany wood, TV-radio, console, 13 channel tuner, 1947, $130.00.

802, 10", mahogany wood, TV-radio/phono, console, 1947, $110.00.

803, 10", mahogany wood, TV-radio, tabletop, 1948, $175.00.

805, 10", Bakelite, tabletop, 1949, $125.00.

806, 10", mahogany wood, tabletop, glass screen, 1949, $75.00.

809, 10", mahogany wood, console, glass screen, 1949, $50.00.

811, 10", mahogany wood, console, glass screen, 1949, $75.00.

807, 10", blond wood, tabletop, glass
screen, 1949, $85.00.

810, 10", mahogany wood, tabletop, 1949, $85.00.

Black & White Television Sets

813, 10", mahogany wood, tabletop, 1949, $70.00.

814, 10", mahogany wood, tabletop, 1949, $70.00.

815, 10", mahogany wood, tabletop, 1949, $40.00.

817, 12", mahogany wood, console, 1949, $40.00.

818, 12", mahogany wood, TV-radio/phono, console, 1949, $30.00.

820, 12", blond wood, TV-radio/phono, console, 1949, $35.00.

821, 12", mahogany wood, tabletop, 1949, $40.00.

830, 12", mahogany wood, tabletop, 1949, $70.00.

835, 10", mahogany wood, tabletop, 1949, $60.00.

840, 12", mahogany wood, TV-radio/phono, console, 1949, $35.00.

901, mahogany wood, TV-radio/phono, projection, console, 1947, $250.00.

910, projection, chassis only, 1947, $50.00.

Hallicrafters

T-54, 7", metal, tabletop, 13 channel push-button tuner, 1948, $150.00.

T-54, 7", metal, tabletop, 12 channel push-button tuner, 1949, $145.00.

T-60, projection, rack-mount, no cabinet, 1948, $60.00.

T-61, 10", Bakelite, tabletop, push-button tuner, 1949, $100.00.

T-64, 10", chassis only, no cabinet, push-button tuner, 1949, $35.00.

T-67, 10", mahogany wood, tabletop, push-button tuner, 1949, $100.00.

Black & White Television Sets

T-68, mahogany wood, projection, console, double doors, 1949, $160.00.

T-69, 15", chassis only, no cabinet, push-button tuner, 1949, $50.00.

T-505, 7", blond wood, tabletop, 13 channel push-button tuner, 1949, $170.00.

T-505, 7", mahogany wood, tabletop, 13 channel push-button tuner, 1949, $160.00.

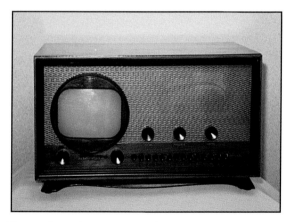

T506, 7", mahogany wood, tabletop, 13 channel push-button tuner, 1948, $170.00.

T-506, 7", mahogany wood, tabletop, 12 channel push-button tuner, 1949, $165.00.

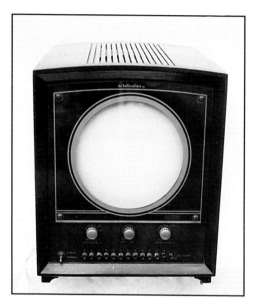

509, 10", wood, tabletop, push-button tuner, 1949, $130.00.

510, 10", Bakelite, tabletop, push-button tuner, 1949, $130.00.

511, 16", two-piece set, control head and speaker separate, 1950, $55.00.

512, 12", wood, console, 1949, $50.00.

514, 7", leatherette, portable, with lid and handle, 1948, $200.00.

515, 15", mahogany wood, console, 1949, $85.00.

Black & White Television Sets

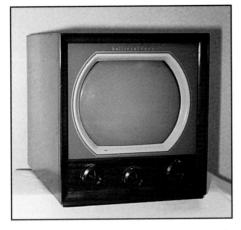

600, 10", mahogany wood, tabletop, 1950, $60.00.

715, 12", Bakelite, tabletop, 1950, $65.00.

716, 12", leatherette, tabletop, 1950, $65.00.

760, 16", wood, console, 1950, $35.00.

761, 16", wood, console, 1950, $35.00.

811, 16", wood, tabletop, rotary tuner, 1950, $50.00.

818, 16", wood, tabletop, rotary tuner, 1950, $75.00.

860, 16", wood, TV-radio/phono, console, double doors, 1950, $50.00.

1005, 20", mahogany wood, console, 1952, $20.00.

1006, 20", blond wood, console, 1952, $50.00.

1056, 21", wood, tabletop, 1952, $20.00.

1075, 21", plastic, tabletop, 1953, $15.00.

1085, 21", wood, console, 1953, $20.00.

Hoffman

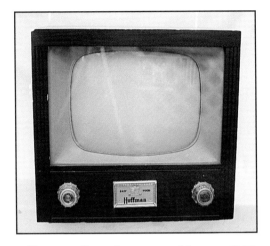

7-M-156, 17", mahogany, tabletop, 1952, $40.00.

600, 10", blond wood, tabletop, 1949, $115.00.

601, 12", mahogany wood, tabletop, 1949, $110.00.

610, 10", blond wood, tabletop, double doors, 1949, $115.00.

611, 10", mahogany wood, tabletop, double doors, 1949, $110.00.

Black & White Television Sets

612, 12", mahogany, wood, tabletop, double doors, 1949, $100.00.

613, 12", blond wood, TV-radio, tabletop, double doors, 1949, $105.00.

841, 12", blond wood, TV-radio, console, double doors, 1949, $70.00.

842, 12", mahogany wood, TV-radio, console, double doors, 1949, $60.00.

843, 12", maple wood, TV-radio, console, double doors, 1949, $60.00.

914, 12", blond wood, TV-radio/phono, console, double doors, 1949, $60.00.

915, 12", mahogany wood, TV-radio/phono, console, double doors, $50.00.

Hotel-Vision

10", wood, tabletop, six channel tuner, 1949, $160.00.

Industrial Television Inc.

IT-1R, 15", metal, tabletop, monitor system, no channel selector, 1948, $50.00.

IT-15R, 7", metal-wood, tabletop, monitor with three channel tuning selector, "GUEST," 1948, $150.00.

IT-22, 10", metal, tabletop, monitor system, no channel selector, 1949, $50.00.

Interstate Stores Television

250, 12", mahogany wood, tabletop, 1950, $65.00.

350, 12", mahogany wood, console, 1950, $40.00.

750, 16", mahogany wood, console, 1950, $40.00.

Jackson Industries

5000, 10", wood, tabletop, 1949, $150.00.

5050, 10", wood, console, 1949, $60.00.

5200, 12", wood, tabletop, 1949, $125.00.

5250, 12", wood, console, 1949, $60.00.

5600, 16", wood, tabletop, 1949, $75.00.

5650, 16", wood, console, 1949, $60.00.

JVC

3020, 5", red and white plastic, transistor, 1978, $35.00.

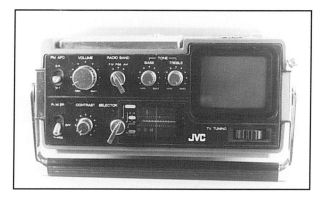

3050, 3", plastic, TV/radio, portable, transistor, 1978, $40.00.

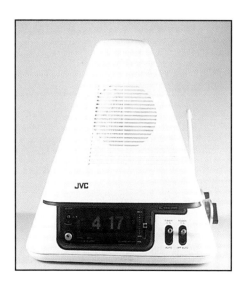

3100D, 6½" white plastic, transistor, with clock, "Pyramid," 1978, $400.00.

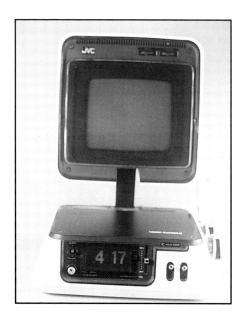

3240, 9", red plastic, transistor, "Videosphere," 1979, $190.00.

3240, 9", white plastic, transistor, "Videosphere," 1979, $150.00.

3241, 9", red plastic, transistor, with clock, "Videosphere," 1979, $190.00.

3241, 9", white plastic, transistor, with clock, "Videosphere," 1979, $140.00.

Magnavox

BF3904BK01, 4", plastic, hand held, transistor, 1987, $45.00.

Majestic

7TV850, 7", wood, tabletop, 12 channel tuner, 1948, $150.00.

12T2, 12", wood, tabletop, 1950, $75.00.

12T3, 12", wood, tabletop, 1950, $75.00.

12C4, 12", wood, console, 1950, $30.00.

12C5, 12", wood, console, 1950, $30.00.

16T2, 14", mahogany wood, tabletop, Bakelite front panel, 1950, $45.00.

16T3, 16", wood, tabletop, 1950, $45.00.

Black & White Television Sets

16C4, 16", wood, console, 1950, $30.00.

16C5, 16", wood, console, 1950, $30.00.

141C, 14", mahogany wood, tabletop, Bakelite front panel, 1951, $40.00.

Mars Television Inc.

630, 16", wood, tabletop, 1949, $65.00.

1200, 12", maple wood, tabletop, 13 channel tuner, 1948, $170.00.

Meck

XB-702, 7", wood, tabletop, 1948, $175.00.

XC-703, 7", leatherette, portable, with lid and handle, 1948, $175.00.

XL-750, 10", wood, tabletop, 1949, $125.00.

XA-701, 7", cloth covered, portable, 1948, $175.00.

XN-752, 10", wood, console, 1949, $100.00.

XQ-776, 12", wood, tabletop, 1949, $80.00.

XQR, 12", wood, TV-radio, tabletop, 1950, $75.00.

XSPS, 16", wood, TV-radio/phono, console, 1950, $40.00.

XTR, 16", wood, TV-radio, tabletop, 1950, $50.00.

Meissner

TV-1, 10", kit, with custom wood cabinet, 1948, $200.00.

TV-24, 12", kit, with custom wood cabinet, 1948, $170.00.

Black & White Television Sets

Merrick Television Co.

Vision Master, 12", blond wood, tabletop, 13 channel tuner, 1949, $150.00.

Mitus Television

2, blond wood, projection, console, "Master," 1948, $190.00.

Motorola

VF-102, 10", wood, TV-radio/phono, console, 13 channel tuner, chassis TS-7, 1948, $75.00.

VF-103M, 10", mahogany wood, TV-radio/phono, console, 12 channel tuner, chassis TS-7, 1948, $100.00.

VK-101, 10", walnut wood, TV-radio, console, 13 channel tuner, chassis TS-5, 1948, $125.00.

VK-101B, 10", blond wood, TV-radio, console, 13 channel tuner, chassis TS-5, 1948, $150.00.

VK-101R, 10", red mahogany wood, console, 13 channel tuner, chassis TS-5, 1948, $125.00.

VK-106, 10", walnut wood, console, chassis TS-9, 1948, $125.00.

VK-106B, 10", blond wood, console, chassis TS-9, 1948, $135.00.

VK-106M, mahogany wood, console, chassis TS-9, 1948, $125.00.

VT-71, 7", walnut wood, tabletop, 13 channel tuner, chassis TS-4D, 1947, $85.00.

VT-71B, 7", blond wood, tabletop, 13 channel tuner, chassis TS-4D, 1948, $100.00.

VT-71M-A, 7", mahogany wood, tabletop, 13 channel tuner, chassis TS4D, 1947, $85.00.

VT-71M-A, 7", mahogany wood, tabletop, 12 channel tuner, chassis TS-4J, 1948, $75.00.

Black & White Television Sets

VT-71MB-A, 7", blond wood, tabletop, 12 channel tuner, chassis TS-4J, 1949, $100.00.

VT-73, 7", tan leatherette, portable, 12 channel tuner, with lid, antenna and handle, chassis TS-4J, 1949, $75.00.

VT-105, 10", walnut wood, tabletop, chassis TS-9, 1948, $180.00.

VT-105M, 10", mahogany wood, tabletop, chassis TS-9, 1948, $180.00.

VT-107, 10", walnut wood, tabletop, chassis TS-9, 1948, $70.00.

VT-107B, 10", blond wood, tabletop, chassis TS-9, 1948, $85.00.

VT-107M, 10", mahogany wood, tabletop, chassis TS-9, 1948, $70.00.

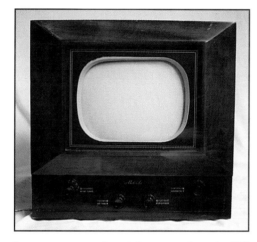

7-VT1R, 7", red mahogany wood, tabletop, chassis TS-18, 1949, $100.00.

7-VT2, 7", Bakelite, tabletop, chassis TS-18, 1949, $125.00.

7-VT-2W, 7", white painted Bakelite, tabletop, chassis TS-18, 1949, $150.00.

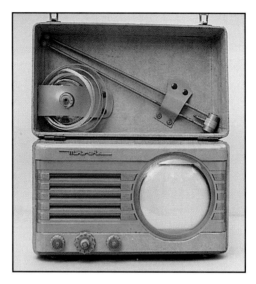

7VT5B, 7", tan leatherette, portable, chassis TS-18, 1949, $85.00.

7VT5R, 7", red leatherette, portable, chassis TS-18, 1949, $95.00.

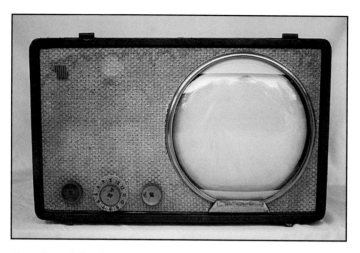

9L1, 8", red leatherette, portable, with lid, chassis TS-18, 1949, $95.00.

9T1, 8", Bakelite, tabletop, chassis TS-18, 1949, $90.00.

9T1S, 8", white painted Bakelite, tabletop, chassis TS-18, 1949, $150.00.

Black & White Television Sets

9VT1, 8", red mahogany wood, tabletop, chassis TS-18, 1949, $100.00.

10T2, 10", walnut wood, tabletop, chassis TS-14, 1950, $95.00.

10T3, 10", red mahogany, tabletop, chassis TS-14, 1950, $95.00.

10VK9B, 10", blond wood, console, chassis TS-9, 1949, $100.00.

10VK9R, 10", red mahogany wood, console, chassis TS-9, 1949, $85.00.

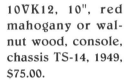

10VK12, 10", red mahogany or walnut wood, console, chassis TS-14, 1949, $75.00.

10VK22R, 10", red mahogany wood, console, chassis TS-14, 1949, $45.00.

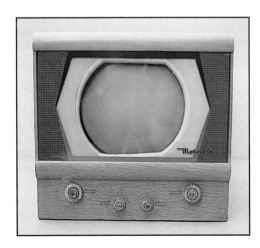

10VT3B, 10", blond wood, tabletop, chassis TS-9, 1949, $100.00.

Black & White Television Sets

10VT3R, 10", red mahogany wood, tabletop, chassis TS-9, 1949, $85.00.

10VT10, 10", walnut wood, tabletop, chassis TS-14, 1949, $65.00.

10VT10B, 10", blond wood, tabletop, chassis TS-14, 1949, $75.00.

10VT24R, 10", red mahogany wood, tabletop, chassis TS-14, 1949, $55.00.

12K1, 12", walnut wood, console, chassis TS-23, 1949, $40.00.

12K1B, 12", blond wood, console, chassis TS-23, 1949, $50.00.

12K2, 12", walnut wood, console, chassis TS-23, 1950, $35.00.

12K2B, 12", blond wood, console, chassis TS-23, 1950, $45.00.

12K3, 12", walnut wood, console, chassis TS-53, 1950, $35.00.

12K3B, 12", blond wood, console, chassis TS-53, 1950, $40.00.

12T1, 12", walnut wood, tabletop, chassis TS-53, 1950, $65.00.

12T1B, 12", blond wood, tabletop, chassis TS-53, 1950, $75.00.

12T2, 12", walnut wood, tabletop, chassis TS-53, 1950, $60.00.

12T2A, 12", mahogany wood, tabletop, chassis TS-53, 1950, $65.00.

12T3, 12", walnut wood, tabletop, chassis TS-53, 1950, $55.00.

12VF4B, 12", blond wood, TV-radio/phono, console, chassis TS-23, 1949, $25.00.

12VF26, 12", mahogany or limed oak wood, TV-radio/phono, console, chassis TS-23, 1950, $30.00.

12VK11, 12", walnut wood, console, chassis TS-23, 1949, $45.00.

12VK11B, 12", limed oak wood, console, chassis TS-23, 1949, $50.00.

12VK11R, 12", red mahogany wood, console, chassis TS-23, 1949, $45.00.

12VT13, 12", walnut wood, tabletop, chassis TS-23, 1950, $65.00.

12VT13B, 12", blond wood, tabletop, chassis TS-23, 1950, $75.00.

Black & White Television Sets

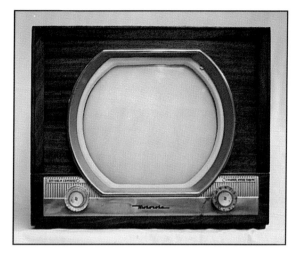

12VT13R, 12", red mahogany wood, tabletop, chassis TS-23, 1950, $65.00.

12VK15R, 12", red mahogany wood, console, double doors, chassis TS-30, 1950, $65.00.

12VK16R, 12", red mahogany wood, console, reverse painted glass screen, chassis TS-30, 1949, $75.00.

12VK18, 12", walnut wood, console, reverse painted glass screen, chassis TS-15, 1949, $75.00.

12VK18B, 12", blond wood, console, reverse painted glass screen, chassis TS-15, 1949, $90.00.

12VT16, 12", walnut wood, tabletop, reverse painted glass screen, chassis TS-15, 1949, $75.00.

14K1, 14", walnut wood, console, chassis TS-88, 1950, $50.00.

16K2L, 16", limed oak wood, console, chassis TS-52, 1950, $45.00.

16VK1B, 16", blond wood, console, chassis TS-52, 1949, $65.00.

16VK1R, 16", red mahogany wood, console, chassis TS-52, 1949, $50.00.

16VK7B, 16", blond wood, console, double doors, chassis TS-16, 1949, $65.00.

16VK7R, 16", red mahogany wood, console, double doors, chassis TS-16, 1949, $50.00.

17F1, 16", walnut wood, TV-radio/phono, console, chassis TS-118, 1950, $30.00.

17F4, 16", walnut wood, TV-radio/phono, console, trundle legs, chassis TS-118, 1950, $35.00.

17F5, 16", walnut wood, TV-radio/phono, console, chassis TS-118, 1950, $30.00.

17K8, 17", walnut wood, console, TS-236, 1951, $45.00.

17K11, 17", walnut wood, console, chassis TS-236, 1951, $45.00.

17K17, 17", walnut wood, console, chassis TS-402, 1953, $40.00.

17T1A, 17", mahogany wood, tabletop, chassis TS-89, 1950, $40.00.

Black & White Television Sets

17T1, 17", walnut wood, tabletop, chassis TS-118, 1950, $50.00.

17T5, 17", Bakelite, tabletop, chassis TS-196, 1951, $35.00.

17T13, 17", Bakelite, tabletop, chassis VTS-408, 1953, $35.00.

17T15, 17", Bakelite, tabletop, chassis VTS-408, 1953, $35.00.

17T16, 17", mahogany wood, tabletop, chassis TS-402, 1954, $25.00.

19K3, 19", mahogany wood, console, double doors, chassis TS-101, 1950, $40.00.

19P1, 19", plastic and metal, portable, "Astronaut," with front cover, 1960, $75.00.

21C2B, 21", blond wood, console, four long spindle legs, TS-502, 1953, $50.00.

21F5, 21", wood, console, TV-radio/phono, chassis TTS-292, 1953, $35.00.

21K12, 21", wood, console, 1954, $30.00.

21K13, 21", wood, console, chassis TS-502, 1953, $30.00.

21K14, 21", wood, console, double doors, chassis QTS-502, 1953, $30.00.

21K15, 21", wood, console, long double doors, chassis QTS-502, 1953, $30.00.

21K16, 21", walnut wood, console, four short spindle legs, chassis QTS-502, 1953, $45.00.

21K17, 21", walnut wood, console, on metal stand, chassis TS-502, 1953, $30.00.

21T8, 21", Bakelite, tabletop, chassis TS-292, 1953, $25.00.

21T10, 21", Bakelite, tabletop, chassis VTS-505, 1953, $25.00.

21T11, 21", walnut wood, tabletop, chassis VTS-502, 1953, $25.00.

24K1, 21", walnut wood, console, chassis TS-602, 1953, $30.00.

24K3, 21", walnut wood console, chassis TS-602, 1954, $30.00.

27K2, 27", walnut wood, console, chassis TS-602, 1953, $35.00.

Black & White Television Sets
Multiple Television Mfg. Co.

MT-1250, 12", mahogany wood, tabletop, 13 channel tuner, 1948, $150.00.

M-1500, 15", mahogany wood, tabletop, 13 channel tuner, 1948, $120.00.

M-2000, 20", mahogany wood, tabletop, 13 channel, tuner, 1948, $130.00.

Muntz

M1, 12", mahogany wood, console, round CRT, 1949, $50.00.

M1, 12", blond wood, console, round CRT, 1949, $55.00.

M30, 12", mahogany wood, tabletop, round CRT, 1950, $60.00.

M31, 16", mahogany wood, tabletop, rectangular CRT, 1950, $25.00.

M31R, 16", mahogany wood, tabletop, round CRT, 1950, $30.00.

M32, 16", mahogany wood, console, round CRT, 1950, $40.00.

17DP, 17", metal, portable, 1959, $35.00.

17PS, 17", metal, portable, 1959, $35.00.

21CP-1, 21", wood, TV-radio/phono, console, 1959, $50.00.

21TB, 21", wood, tabletop, 1959, $25.00.

21TM, 21", wood, tabletop, 1959, $25.00.

24CB, 24", wood, console, 1959, $50.00.

24CM, 24", wood, console, 1959, $50.00.

National

TV-7M, 7", metal, tabletop, 1949, $240.00.

TV-7W, 7", mahogany wood, tabletop, 1949, $240.00.

TV-10T, 10", mahogany wood, tabletop, 1949, $160.00.

TV-7M, 7", metal, with Video-Meter, tabletop, 1949, $350.00.

TV-10W, 10", mahogany wood, tabletop, 1949, $170.00.

TV-12W, 12", mahogany wood, tabletop, 1949, $120.00.

TV-1201, 12", mahogany wood, tabletop, 1949, $100.00.

TV-1225, 12", wood, console, 1949, $75.00.

TV-1226, 12", wood, console, 1949, $75.00.

TV-1601, 16", wood, tabletop, 1949, $65.00.

TV-1625, 16", wood, console, 1949, $60.00.

New England Television Co.

Direct View Custom Console, 15", wood, console, 1949, $100.00.

Neilsen Television Corp.

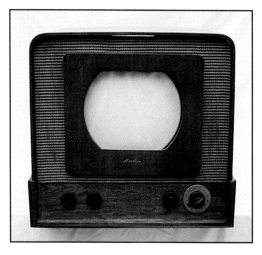

1010, 10", wood, tabletop, 1949, $160.00.

1018, 10", wood, console, 1949, $85.00.

Black & White Television Sets

Norelco
(North American Philips Company)

Protelgram, projection system conversion kit, without cabinet, 1948, $20.00.

PA-2A, wood, projection, console, internal and external projection system, "Due-Vue," 1949, $85.00.

PT-200, wood, projection, console, 1948, $70.00.

PT-300, wood, projection, console, 1948, double doors, $75.00.

Olympic

DX-214, 12", wood, tabletop, 1949, $55.00.

DX-215, 12", wood, console, double doors, 1949, $45.00.

DX-216, 12", wood, console, 1949, $50.00.

DX-619, 16", wood, console, double doors, 1950, $40.00.

DX-620, 16", wood, console, 1950, $45.00.

DX-621, 16", wood, TV-radio/phono, console, $75.00.

DX-931, 19", wood, console, double doors, 1950, $40.00.

DX-932, 19", wood, console, 1950, $45.00.

DX-950, 16", wood, tabletop, 1950, $65.00.

TV-104, 10", wood, tabletop, "Cruzair," 1948, $80.00.

TV-105, 10", wood, console, 1948, $65.00.

TV-106, 10", wood, tabletop, 1948, $80.00.

TV-107, 10", wood, tabletop, 1948, $75.00.

TV-108, 10", wood, tabletop, 1948, $60.00.

TV922, 10", mahogany wood, tabletop, "Pace-maker," 1948, $85.00.

TV-922L, 10", wood, tabletop, "Deluxe Ten," 1948, $120.00.

TV-928, 10", wood, TV-radio/phono, console, with mirror in top lid, 1948, $120.00.

TV-944, 12", wood, tabletop, "Beverly," 1949, $75.00.

Black & White Television Sets

TV-945, 12", wood, console, "Plaza," 1949, $75.00.

TV-946, 12", wood, tabletop, 1949, $75.00.

TV-947, 16", wood, console, double doors, 1949, $30.00.

RTU-3, 10", wood, remote monitor, tabletop, 1949, $75.00.

752, 16", wood, tabletop, 1950, $40.00.

753, 16", wood, console, 1950, $40.00.

755, 16", wood, console, 1950, $30.00.

Packard Bell

1080TV, 10", blond wood, TV-radio/phono, console, double doors, 1949, $50.00.

1091TV, 10", mahogany wood, TV-radio/phono, console, double doors, 1949, $35.00.

1291TV, 12", blond wood, TV-radio/phono player and recorder, console, 1949, $45.00.

2001TV, 12", blond wood, tabletop, 1949, $85.00.

2002TV, 12", blond wood, console, "Telecaster," 1949, $45.00.

2091, 12", mahogany wood, tabletop, 1949, $60.00.

2092TV, 12", mahogany wood, console, "Telecaster," 1949, $40.00.

2291TV, 10", blond wood, console, single door, "Telecaster," 1949, $65.00.

2292TV, 10", blond wood, console, "Consolette," 1949, $75.00.

2293TV, 10", mahogany wood, tabletop, 1949, $95.00.

2294TV, 12", mahogany wood, tabletop, 1949, $75.00.

2295TV, 12", blond wood, console, single door, "Telecaster," 1949, $55.00.

2296TV, 12", blond, wood, console, "Consolette," 1949, $65.00.

2297TV, 12", mahogany wood, console, double doors, "De Luxe," 1949, $40.00.

2297TV, 12", mahogany wood, console, "Standard," 1949, $45.00.

2298TV, 12", mahogany wood, tabletop, 1949, $75.00.

2991TV, 16", mahogany wood, console, double doors, "Telecaster," 1949, $50.00.

3191TV, 10", blond wood, console, single door, 1949, $65.00.

3192TV, 10", mahogany wood, console, 1949, $60.00.

3193TV, 10", mahogany wood, tabletop, 12 channel tuner, 1949, $90.00.

Black & White Television Sets

3194TV, 10", walnut wood, tabletop, 12 channel tuner 1948, $90.00.

3381, 10", mahogany wood, console, 12 channel tuner, "Telecaster," 1948, $80.00.

4580, 12", TV-radio/phono player and phono recorder, 13 channel tuner, 1948, $125.00.

Panasonic

CT-101, 1½", LCD, transistor, color, with accessories, 1980, $150.00.

TR-001, 1½", plastic, portable, transistor, 1974, $350.00.

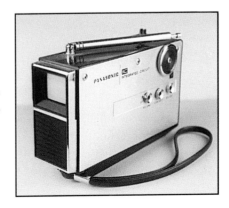

TR-003, 3", plastic, TV/radio, transistor, portable, 1975, $50.00.

TR-005, 5", transistor, tabletop, "Flying Saucer," 1975, $350.00.

TR-435R, 5", TV-radio, transistor, portable, 1976, $20.00.

TR-475, 5", TV-radio, transistor, portable, pop-up screen, 1977, $20.00.

TR-535, 5", TV-radio, transistor, portable, 1977, $30.00.

TR-545, 5", TV-radio, transistor, pop-up screen, 1977, $30.00.

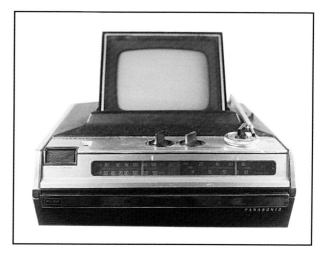

TR-425R, 5", TV-radio, portable, transistor, 1976, $30.00.

TR-729, 8", transistor, portable, 1977, $25.00.

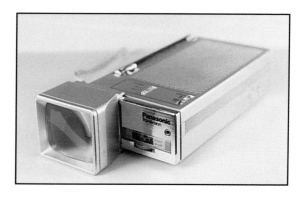

TR-1010P, 1½", plastic, portable, transistor, with magnifier, 1981, $70.00.

TR-1020P, 1½", TV-radio, transistor, portable, 1981, $50.00.

TR-1030C, 1½", plastic, portable, with magnifier, 1984, $60.00.

TR-3000P, 3", TV-radio, portable, transistor, 1980, $100.00.

Black & White Television Sets

Pathè

12-1, 12", mahogany wood, tabletop, 1948, $350.00.

Philco

B-350-HYL, 9", yellow plastic, tabletop, transistor, 1982, $75.00.

B-370-ETG, 9", red plastic, tabletop, transistor, 1982, $60.00.

B-370-FWH, 9", white plastic, tabletop, transistor, 1982, $50.00.

H2010L, 2", tan leather, transistor, with hood, "Safari," $170.00.

H2010BL, 2", black leather, transistor, with hood, "Safari," $170.00.

48-700, 7", mahogany wood, tabletop, 1948, $190.00.

48-1000, 10", mahogany wood, tabletop, 1948, $300.00.

Black & White Television Sets

48-1001, 10", mahogany wood, tabletop, 1948, $125.00.

48-1050, 10", wood, console, 1948, $100.00.

48-2500, wood, projection, console, 1948, $125.00.

49-702, 7", wood, tabletop, 1949, $200.00.

49-1002, 10", wood, tabletop, 1949, $80.00.

49-1040, 10", mahogany wood, console, tall wood legs, 1949, $65.00.

49-1076, 10", wood, TV-radio/phono, console, double doors, 1949, $50.00.

49-1150, 10", blond wood, console, tall wood legs, $75.00.

49-1150, 10", mahogany wood, console, tall wood legs, $70.00.

49-1240, 12", wood, console, tall wood legs, 1949, $50.00.

49-1280, 12", wood, console, double doors, 1949, $50.00.

49-1443-M, 14", mahogany wood, console, tall wood legs, 1949, $50.00.

49-1443-B, 14", blond wood, tall wood legs, 1949, $70.00.

49-1475, 14", wood, console, double doors, 1949, $50.00.

49-1477, 14", wood, TV-radio/phono, console, 1949, $40.00.

49-1630, 16", mahogany wood, console, double doors, 1949, $40.00.

50-701, 7", black Bakelite, tabletop, 1950, $200.00.

50-701, 7", brown Bakelite, tabletop, 1950, $200.00.

50-702, 7", red mahogany wood, tabletop, 1950, $180.00.

50-T1104, 10", Bakelite, tabletop, 1950, $85.00.

50-T1403, 12", mahogany wood, tabletop, round top cabinet, 1950, $65.00.

Black & White Television Sets

50-T-1404, 12", mahogany wood, tabletop, 1950, $40.00.

50-T-1443, 14", mahogany wood, console, tall wood legs, 1950, $80.00.

50-T1600, 16", mahogany wood, tabletop, 1950, $15.00.

51-T1601, 16", metal, tabletop, 1951, $35.00.

51-T1634, 16", wood, console, 1951, $20.00.

51-T1871, 20", wood, TV-radio/phono, console, 1951, $15.00.

51-T-1872, 20", wood, TV-radio/phono, console, 1951, $15.00.

50-T1632, 16", mahogany wood, console, 1950, $35.00.

51-T-1607, 16", metal, tabletop, 1951, $35.00.

Philco Predicta

Notice: Predicta prices vary widely!
Due to the popularity explosion of these sets, prices will vary to the extreme. The following prices are for clean and complete non-working sets.

UG-3408, 17", metal, tabletop, with cloth grille, "Debutante," 1960, $200.00.

UG-3410, 17", metal, tabletop, with metal grille, "Princess," 1960, $200.00.

UG-3412, 17", metal, tabletop, with clock in grille, "Siesta," 1960, $230.00.

UG-4240, 21", gray metal, tabletop, 1959, $25.00.

UG-4242M, 21", mahogany wood, tabletop, "Holiday," 1958, $200.00.

UG-4242L, 21", blond wood, tabletop, "Holiday," 1958, $300.00.

UG-4654M, 21", mahogany wood, console, "Barber-pole," 1958, $400.00.

UG-4654L, 21", blond wood, console, "Barber-pole," 1958, $500.00.

UG-4658SM, 21", mahogany wood and metal, console, swivel base, "Miss America," 1960, $100.00.

Black & White Television Sets

UG-4658SL, 21", blond wood and metal, console, swivel base, "Miss America," 1960, $110.00.

UG-4660SM, 21", blond wood, console, swivel base, "Miss America," 1960, $100.00.

UG-4662-P, 21", mahogany wood, corner console, 1960, $40.00.

UG-4682, 21", wood, console, swivel base, "Riviera," 1960, $65.00.

UG-4710, 21", blond wood, console, two piece, screen on long cord, "Penthouse," 1959, $350.00.

UG-4720, 21", mahogany wood, console, four knobs on top back for stereo controls, four legs, two piece, screen on long cord, "Stereophonic Tandem," 1960, $400.00.

UG-4730, 21", mahogany wood, console, four fin shaped legs, "Continental," 1960, $500.00.

123

Black & White Television Sets

UG-4744, 21", wood, console, "Townhouse," 1960, $500.00.

UG-6628L, 24", blond wood, console, swivel base, 1960, $55.00.

UG-6632M, 24", mahogany wood, console, swivel base, 1960, 60.00.

Philharmonic Radio Corp.

1049, 10", mahogany wood, tabletop, 1949, $80.00.

1249, 12", mahogany wood, tabletop, 1949, $70.00.

5000, 10", mahogany wood, tabletop, 1950, $75.00.

Philmore Mfg. Co.

P30, 10", wood, console, 13 channel tuner, 1948, $100.00.

Pilot

TV-37, 3", wood-press board, tabletop, 1947, $175.00, with case 200.00, with case and magnifier $250.00.

TV-125, 12", wood, TV-radio, tabletop, 1949, $75.00.

TV-161, 16", wood, TV-radio, tabletop, 1950, $60.00.

TV-950, wood, projection, console, 1949, $90.00.

TV-952, wood, projection, TV-radio/phono, console, 1949, $125.00.

RCA

T-100, 10", metal, tabletop, 1949, $30.00.

T-120, 12", metal, tabletop, 1949, $20.00.

T-121, 12", metal, tabletop, 1949, $20.00.

T-164, 16", mahogany wood, tabletop, 1950, $35.00.

TC-165, 16", mahogany wood, console, 1950, $30.00.

Black & White Television Sets

TC-167, 16", mahogany wood, console, double doors, 1950, $30.00.

TLS-86, wood, projection, console, 1946, $150.00.

2T51, 12", metal, tabletop, 1950, $50.00.

2T60, 12", wood, tabletop, 1950, $55.00.

2T81, 12", wood, TV-radio/phono, console, 1950, $45.00.

4T101, 14", wood, tabletop, 1951, $15.00.

6PTK48, mahogany wood, projection, TV-radio, console, 1946, $250.00.

6T54, 16", wood, console, 1950, $40.00.

6T64, 16", wood, console, 1950, $40.00.

6T65, 16", wood, console, 1950, $40.00.

6T75, 16", wood, console, double doors, 1950, $40.00.

6T84, 16", wood, TV-radio/phono, console, 1950, $40.00.

6T86, 16", wood, TV-radio/phono, console, 1950, $40.00.

6T87, 16", wood, TV-radio/phono, console, 1950, $40.00.

7T112, 17", wood, console, 1951, $25.00.

6T71, 16", wood, console, double doors, 1950, $40.00.

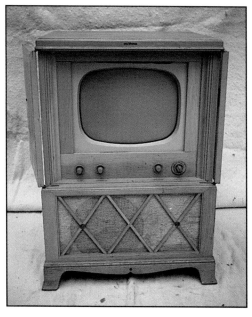

7T122, 17", blond wood, console, double doors, 1951, $40.00.

7T124, 17", mahogany wood, console, 1951, $25.00.

8PCS41, blond wood, projection, console, lift-up screen, 13 channel tuner, 1948, $125.00.

8-PT-7010, 8", metal, portable, 1956, $35.00.

8-PT-7011, 8", metal, portable, 1956, $35.00.

8-PT-7030, 8", metal, portable, with swivel base, 1956, $50.00.

8-PT-7031, 8", metal, portable, with swivel base, 1956, $50.00.

8T241, 10", mahogany wood, tabletop, 1948, $90.00.

8T243, 10", wood, tabletop, 1948, $90.00.

8T244, 10" mahogany wood, tabletop, double doors, 1948, $75.00.

8T270, 16", mahogany wood, tabletop, 1949, $55.00.

8TC271, 16", wood, console, Queen Anne style cabinet, double doors, 1949, $170.00.

8TK29, 10", wood, TV-radio, console, 1949, $125.00.

8TR29, 10", wood, TV-radio, console, 1949, $125.00.

8TS30, 10", mahogany wood, tabletop, 1949, $100.00.

8TV321, 10", wood, TV-radio, console, double doors, 1949, $75.00.

8TV323, 10", wood, TV-radio, console, double doors, 1949, $75.00.

9PC41, mahogany wood, projection, console, lift-up screen, 13 channel tuner, 1949, $125.00.

9T57, 19", wood, Consolette, 1951, $25.00.

9T77, 19", wood, console, double doors, 1950, $30.00.

9T79, 19", wood, console, double doors, 1950, $30.00.

9T89, 19", wood, TV-radio/phono, console, 1950, $30.00.

9T256, 10", metal, tabletop, 1949, $75.00.

9TC245, 12", wood, console, 1949, $40.00.

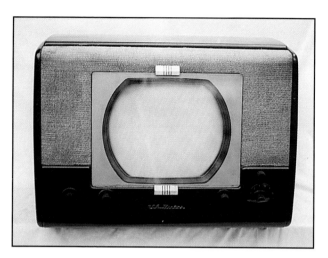

9T246, 10", metal, tabletop, 1949, $40.00.

9TC247, 12", wood, console, 1949, $40.00.

14-PD-3030, 14", metal, portable, 1954, $20.00.

Black & White Television Sets

17-S-1632, 17", metal, tabletop, 1956, $35.00.

17-T-211, 17", wood, console, 1953, $20.00.

17-T-220, 17", wood, console, 1953, $20.00.

21-D-368, 21", wood, console, 1953, $20.00.

21-D-379, 21", wood, console, 1953, $20.00.

21-S-354, 21", wood, console, 1953, $15.00.

21-S-357, 21", wood, console, 1953, $15.00.

21-T-313, 21", wood, console, 1953, $10.00.

21-T-314, 21", wood, console, 1953, $10.00.

21-T-316, 21", wood, console, 1953, $10.00.

21-T-322, 21", wood, console, double doors, 1953, $20.00.

21-T-323, 21", wood, console, double doors, 1953, $20.00.

21-T-324, 21", wood, console, double doors, $20.00.

621TS, 7", mahogany or walnut wood, tabletop, 1946, $450.00.

621TS, 7", blond wood, tabletop, 1946, $550.00.

630TCS, 10", mahogany wood, console, 1946, $400.00.

630TS, 10", mahogany wood, tabletop, 1946, $175.00.

Black & White Television Sets

641TV, 10", wood, TV-radio/phono, console, 1947, $125.00.

648PTK, wood, projection, TV-radio, console, 1947, $150.00.

648PV, wood, projection, console, $125.00.

721TCS, 10", wood, console, 1947, $100.00.

721TS, 10", wood, tabletop, 1947, $90.00.

730TV1, 10", mahogany wood, TV/radio-phono, console, double doors, 1947, $75.00.

730TV2, 10", wood, console, double doors, 1947, $75.00.

741PCS, wood, projection, console, 1947, $350.00.

Raytheon-Belmont

7DX21, 7", mahogany wood, tabletop, sold under many other names, 1948, $120.00.

7DX22-P, 7", cloth-covered, portable, 1948, $125.00.

Black & White Television Sets

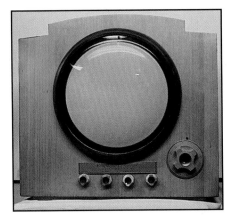

10DX21, 10", mahogany wood, console, slide out screen, "Observer," 948, $80.00.

10DX22, 10", mahogany wood, console, slide out screen, 1948, $80.00.

10DX24, 10", mahogany wood, tabletop, 1948, $90.00.

10DX24, 10", blond wood, tabletop, 1948, $100.00.

18DX21, 7", mahogany wood, tabletop, sold under many other names, 1948, $120.00.

21A21, 7", wood, tabletop, 1947, $200.00.

22AX22, 10", wood, console, 1947, $150.00.

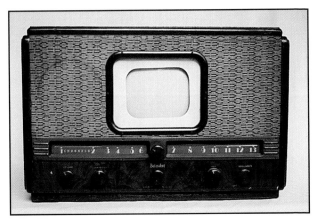

22AX21, 7", wood, tabletop, 1947, $200.00.

C-1104-B, 12", mahogany wood, console, chassis 12AX27, 1949, $80.00.

C-1105, 12", mahogany wood, console, 1949, $85.00.

M-1101, 12", wood, tabletop, 1949, $120.00.

M-1105, 12", mahogany wood, tabletop, chassis 12AX27, 1949, $110.00.

M-1106, 12", maroon Bakelite, tabletop, chassis 12AX27, 1950, $40.00.

M-1107, 12", blond Bakelite, tabletop, chassis 12AX27, 1950, $40.00.

M1401, 16", mahogany wood, console, chassis 14AX21, 1950, $25.00.

M1402, 16", mahogany wood, tabletop, chassis 14AX21, 1950, $25.00.

M-1601, 16", mahogany wood, console, chassis 16AX23, 1950, $125.00.

Black & White Television Sets

Realistic

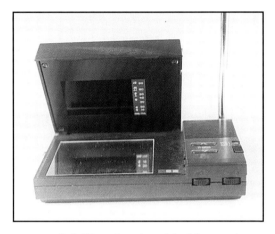

16-157, 2", LCD color, hand held, transistor, 1990, $50.00.

Regal

1007, 10", mahogany wood, tabletop, 1948, $90.00.

1207, 12", mahogany wood, table top, 1948, $80.00.

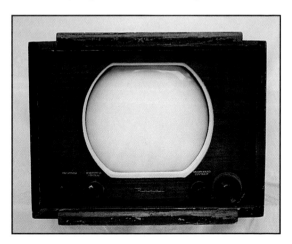

1208, 12", mahogany wood, console, 1948, $75.00.

1230, 12", maple wood, tabletop, 1948, $100.00.

1607, 16", walnut wood, tabletop, 1949, $60.00.

16T31, 16", mahogany wood, tabletop, 1949, $60.00.

16T36, 16", mahogany wood, TV-radio, tabletop, 1949, $60.00.

Scott

6T11, wood, projection, tabletop, 1949, $200.00.

13-A 12", mahogany wood, console, double doors, 1947, $600.00.

300, 10", mahogany wood, console, double doors, 1948, $200.00.

400A, wood, projection, tabletop, 1948, $300.00.

800BT, wood, projection, TV-radio/phono, console, 1949, $400.00.

Silvertone (Sears, Roebuck & Company)

101, 12", mahogany wood, tabletop, 1949, $40.00.

101A, 12", mahogany wood, TV-radio/phono, console, double doors, 1949, $30.00.

112, 12", walnut wood, tabletop, 1949, $35.00.

125B, 10", mahogany wood, tabletop, 1949, $75.00.

132, 12", blond wood, console, 1949, $65.00.

133, 12", mahogany wood, tabletop, 1949, $55.00.

137, 12", walnut wood, TV-radio/phono, console, double doors, 1949, $30.00.

8130, 7", mahogany wood, tabletop, 1949, $140.00.

8132, 10", walnut wood, tabletop, push-button, tuner, 1948, $90.00.

8133, 10", mahogany wood, TV-radio, tabletop, push-button tuner, 1948, $75.00.

9111, 10", walnut wood, tabletop, 1949, $60.00.

9112, 12", walnut wood, tabletop, 1949, $55.00.

9113, 10", mahogany wood, tabletop, 1949, $60.00.

9114, 12", mahogany wood, tabletop, 1949, $55.00.

9115, 8", leatherette, portable, 1949, $130.00.

9116, 7", leatherette, portable, 1949, $120.00.

9120, 12", mahogany wood, tabletop, 1949, $40.00.

9121, 12", walnut wood, tabletop, double doors, push-button tuner, 1949, $50.00.

9122, 12", mahogany wood, console, double doors, push-button tuner, $70.00.

9123, 10", mahogany wood, tabletop, 1949, $50.00.

9124, 12", mahogany wood, tabletop, 1949, $45.00.

9125B, 10", brown Bakelite, tabletop, 1949, $75.00.

Black & White Television Sets

9126, 12", mahogany wood, console, 1949, $40.00.

9127, 12", walnut wood, console, 1949, $40.00.

9128, 12", blond wood, console, double doors, push-button tuner, $65.00.

9129, 10", walnut, console, 1949, $60.00.

9130, 12", mahogany wood, console, 1949, $50.00.

9131, 10", wood, tabletop, 1949, $110.00.

9132, 12", blond wood, console, 1949, $65.00.

9133, 10", wood, TV-radio/phono, console, 1949, $35.00.

9134, 12", wood, TV-radio/phono, console, 1949, $35.00.

9135, 16", mahogany wood, console, 1949, $45.00.

9139, 12", walnut wood, console, 1949, $40.00.

9140, 12", mahogany wood, console, 1949, $40.00.

Setchel Carlson

C-105, 17", metal, leatherette covered, tabletop, 1956, $30.00.

Seiko

TR-02-01, 1", LCD, TV-radio,
"TV Watch," 1990, $400.00.

Black & White Television Sets

Sentinel

400TV, 7", black cloth-covered, portable, 1948, $115.00.

400TV, 7", tan cloth-covered, portable, 1948, $125.00.

401TVM, 10", wood, tabletop, 1948, $75.00.

402, 10", wood, console, 1948, $60.00.

405, 7", wood, tabletop, 1948, $100.00.

406TVM, 12", wood, tabletop, 1948, $85.00.

407TVM, 16", wood, console, 1948, $65.00.

409TVM, 16", wood, console, 1948, $55.00.

411CVM, 12", wood, console, 1948, $50.00.

412, 10", wood, tabletop, 1949, $60.00.

415-CV, 12", mahogany wood, tabletop, 1949, $55.00.

416, 12", wood, console, 1949, $35.00.

419, 19", wood, console, 1949, $45.00.

429-TV, 16", wood, tabletop, 1951, $20.00.

431-TV, 16", wood, console, 1951, $20.00.

1201, 12", mahogany wood, tabletop, 1950, $65.00.

Sharp

AA-101W, 5", white plastic, tabletop, transistor, 1983, $40.00.

3-S-111R, 5", red plastic, tabletop, transistor, 1981, $60.00.

3-T-50C, 4", portable, transistor, "Sidekick," 1982, $60.00.

Singer

TV-A-6, 5", transistor, portable, AC-DC, VHF, with case and accessories, 1963, $55.00.

TV-A-6U, 5", transistor, portable, AC-DC, VHF-UHF, with case and accessories, 1963, $65.00.

Sinclair

MTV-1, 1¾", transistor, portable, with accessories, 1979, $160.00.

Black & White Television Sets

Snaider (See Television Assembly Co.)

Sony

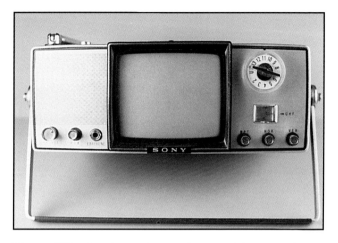

BP-6, 3½", plastic and metal, portable, transistor, 1965, $65.00.

FD-10A, 2", gray plastic, LCD, transistor, "Watchman," 1989, $45.00.

Sony

FD-10A, 2", blue plastic, LCD, transistor, "Watchman," 1989, $55.00.

FD-42A, 2", white plastic, LCD, transistor, "Watchman," 1989, $55.00.

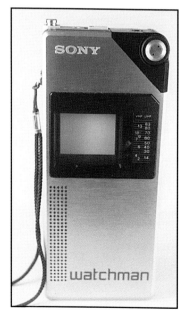

FD-210, 1¾", plastic, transistor, "Watchman," 1988, $140.00.

Black & White Television Sets

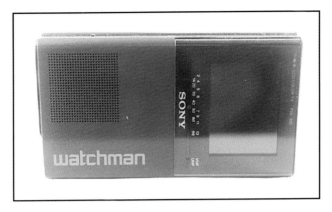

FDL-310, 2½", gray plastic, transistor, "Watchman," 1988, $120.00.

FDL-3500, 3", color, portable, transistor, 1989, $250.00.

KV-4000, 3½", color, portable, transistor, 1989, $500.00.

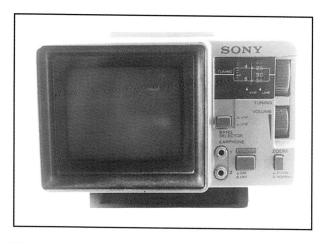

TV-415, 3½", plastic, portable, transistor, 1989, $35.00.

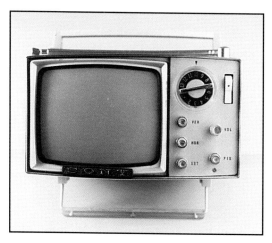

5-303W, 5", transistor, portable, AC-DC, VHF, 1964, $65.00.

5-303UW, 5", transistor, portable, AC-DC, VHF, 1964, $50.00.

Black & White Television Sets

5-305, 5", transistor, portable, AC-DC, VHF, 1965, $50.00.

5-307UW, 5", transistor, used in hospital, AC-DC, VHF only, "STERICALL," 1965, $75.00.

5-307UW, 5", transistor, portable, AC-DC, VHF-UHF, 1965, $50.00.

8-301W, 8", transistor, portable, AC-DC, 1961, $275.00.

Sparton

4900-TV, 12", mahogany wood, TV-radio, console, mirror in lid, 1949, $110.00.

4901-TV, 12", blond wood, TV-radio, console, mirror in lid, 1949, $120.00.

4916-TV, 10", wood, TV-radio/phono, console, 1949, $75.00.

4917, 10", mahogany wood, TV-radio/phono, console, 1949, $75.00.

4918, 10", blond wood, TV-radio/phono, console, 1949, $90.00.

4920, 12", wood, console, double doors, 1949, $60.00.

4931, 10", wood, console, 1949, $80.00.

4935, 12", wood, console, 1949, $60.00.

4939-TV, 12", walnut wood, TV-radio, console, mirror in lid, 1949, $120.00.

4940-TV, 10", mahogany wood, TV-radio, console, mirror in lid, 1949, $130.00.

4941-TV, 10", blond wood, console, mirror in lid, 1949, $140.00.

4951, 10", mahogany, wood, tabletop, 1949, $115.00.

4952, 10", blond wood, tabletop, 1949, $125.00.

Black & White Television Sets

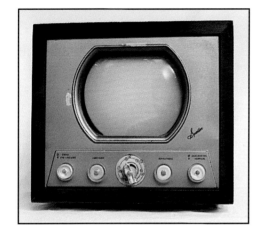

4954, 10", mahogany wood, tabletop, 1949, $110.00.

4960, 12", wood, tabletop, 1949, $85.00.

4964, 16", wood, console, double doors, 1949, $60.00.

4965, 16", wood, console, double doors, 1949, $60.00.

5002, 10", wood, tabletop, 1950, $75.00.

5003, 10", wood, tabletop, 1950, $75.00.

5006, 10", wood, tabletop, 1950, $75.00.

5007, 10", wood, tabletop, 1950, $75.00.

5010, 10", wood, tabletop, 1950, $75.00.

5011, 12", wood, tabletop, 1950, $65.00.

5056, 12", wood, console, 1950, $65.00.

5057, 12", wood, console, 1950, $65.00.

5220, 17", leatherette, tabletop, 1952, $50.00.

5225, 17", wood, tabletop, 1952, $60.00.

5226, 17", wood, tabletop, 1952, $60.00.

5262, 17", wood, console, 1952, $30.00.

5263, 17", wood, console, 1952, $30.00.

5265, 17", wood, console, double doors, 1953, $30.00.

24542, 27", wood, console, 1953, $25.00.

25544, 27", wood, console, 1953, $25.00.

26542, 27", wood, console, 1953, $25.00.

52412, 24", wood, console, 1953, $25.00.

52413, 24", wood, console, 1953, $20.00.

56412, 24", wood, console, 1953, $25.00.

56413, 24", wood, console, 1953, $25.00.

Starrette

Ambassador, 16", wood, tabletop, 1949, $125.00.

Adams, 12", wood, TV-radio/phono, console, 1949, $40.00.

Chinese Hancock, 16", wood, TV-radio/phono, console, 1949, $100.00.

Black & White Television Sets

Cleveland, 16", wood, TV-radio/phono, console, 1949, $50.00.

Cosmopolitan, 16", wood, TV-radio/phono, console, 1949, $125.00.

Gotham, 16", wood, TV-radio/phono, console, 1949, $30.00.

Henry Hudson, 16", wood, tabletop, 1949, $50.00.

Henry Parks, 16", wood, console, 1949, $40.00.

Jackson, 16", wood, TV-radio, console, 1949, $100.00.

Jefferson, 12", wood, console, double doors, 1949, $110.00.

John Hancock, 16", wood, TV-radio/phono, console, 1949, $45.00.

King Arthur, 20", wood, console, 1949, $75.00.

Lincoln, 16", wood, TV-radio/phono, console, 1949, $45.00.

Nathan Hale, 12", wood, tabletop, 1949, $100.00.

Stewart-Warner

T-711, 10", wood, TV-radio, console, 13 channel tuner, 1948, $80.00.

T-712, 10", wood, TV-radio, console, 13 channel tuner, 1948, $80.00.

21T-9300H, 21", leatherette, tabletop, 1953, $15.00.

27C-9212, 27", wood, console, 1953, $10.00.

9054-A, 10", mahogany wood, console, long wood legs, "AVT-1," 1948, $60.00.

9054-B, 10", blond oak wood, console, mirror in lid, "AVC-2," 1948, $135.00.

9054-C, 10", mahogany wood, console, mirror in lid, "AVC-3," 1948, $125.00.

9100-A, 10", mahogany wood, tabletop, double doors, 1949, $75.00.

9100-B, 10", mahogany wood, console, mirror in lid, 1949, $100.00.

Black & White Television Sets

9100-C, 10", maple wood, console, mirror in lid, 1949, $100.00.

9100-D, 10", walnut wood, console, mirror in lid, 1949, $100.00.

9100-E, 10", mahogany wood, tabletop, 1949, $75.00.

9120-A, 16", mahogany wood, tabletop, 1950, $35.00.

9120-B, 16", mahogany wood, console, 1950, $30.00.

9120-C, 16", mahogany wood, console, long double doors, 1950, $30.00.

9120-D, 16", mahogany wood, console, double doors, 1950, $30.00.

9120-E, 16", blond wood, console, double doors, 1950, $35.00.

9120-F, 16", blond wood, console, double doors, 1950, $35.00.

9121-B, 17", wood, TV-radio/phono, console, 1951, $15.00.

9126, 17", wood, tabletop, 1951, $15.00.

9127, 17", wood, console, 1951, $15.00.

9200-A, 14", mahogany wood, tabletop, leatherette front panel, 1950, $50.00.

Stromberg-Carlson

TC-10, 10", wood, tabletop, 1949, $140.00.

TC-19-LM, 19", wood, console, 1949, $50.00.

TC-125-HM, 12", wood, tabletop, $120.00.

TC-125-LA, 12", wood, console, 1949, $100.00.

TS-16-L1, 16", mahogany wood, TV-radio, console, 1949, $75.00.

TS-16-PM, 16", wood, TV-radio/phono, console, double doors, 1949, $75.00.

TS-125-LM, 12", wood, TV-radio, console, 1949, $65.00.

TV-10-L, 10", wood, tabletop, seven channel push-button tuner, 1947, $265.00.

TV-10-P, 10", wood, TV-radio/phono, console, seven channel push-button tuner, 1947, $200.00.

TV-12-H2, 12", wood, tabletop, 1947, $125.00.

Black & White Television Sets

TV-12-LM, 12", wood, console, double doors, 1947, $75.00.

TV-12-M5M, 12", wood, TV-radio/phono, console, double doors, 1947, $85.00.

TV-12-PGM, 12", wood, TV-radio/phono, console, double doors, 1947, $50.00.

TV-125-LM, 12", wood, TV-radio, console, 1948, $65.00.

317-RPM, 17", wood, TV-radio/phono, console, 1951, $35.00.

421-CDM, 21", wood, console, double doors, 1952, $20.00.

421-CM, 21", wood, console, 1952, $15.00.

421-TX, 21", wood, tabletop, 1952, $20.00.

Sylvania

1-075, 10", mahogany wood, tabletop, chassis 1-139, 1950, $55.00.

1-076, 10", mahogany wood, TV-radio/phono, console, chassis 1-108, 1950, $30.00.

1-090, 16", mahogany wood, console, double doors, chassis 1-168, 1950, $35.00.

1-113, 12", mahogany wood, console, chassis 1-139, 1950, $35.00.

1-114, 12", walnut wood, console, chassis 1-139, 1950, $35.00.

1-124, 12", mahogany wood, tabletop, chassis 1-139, 1950, $40.00.

1-125, 12", walnut wood, tabletop, chassis 1-139, 1950, $40.00.

1-125-1, 12", mahogany wood, tabletop, chassis 1-139, 1950, $35.00.

1-128, 16", mahogany wood, TV-radio/phono, console, chassis 1-108, 1950, $30.00.

1-177, 12", walnut wood, tabletop, chassis 1-186, 1950, $30.00.

1-197, 12", mahogany wood, console, double doors, chassis 1-139, $40.00.

1-197-1, 12", mahogany wood, console double doors, chassis 1-186, 1950, $40.00.

1-197-2, 12", mahogany wood, console, double doors, chassis 1-227, 1951, $35.00.

1-210, 10", blond wood, tabletop, chassis 1-139, 1950, $50.00.

1-245, 12", mahogany wood, console, chassis 1-139, 1950, $40.00.

1-245-1, 12", mahogany wood, console, chassis 1-186, 1950, $40.00.

1-245-2, 12", mahogany wood, console, chassis 1-227, 1951, $35.00.

1-246, 12", mahogany wood, tabletop, chassis 1-138, 1950, $35.00.

1-246-1, 12", mahogany wood, tabletop, chassis 1-186, 1950, $35.00.

1-247, 16", mahogany wood, console, chassis 1-168, 1950, $35.00.

1-247-1, 16", mahogany wood, console, chassis 1-231, 1950, $35.00.

14P101, 14", metal, portable, 1957, $25.00.

14P102, 14", metal, portable, 1957, $35.00.

21C405, 21", wood, console, "Halolight," 1959, $100.00.

21C529, 21", limed oak wood, console, "Halolight," 1959, $170.00.

21C534, 21", wood, console, "Halolight," 1959, $125.00.

21C607M, 21", mahogany wood, console, "Halolight," 1959, $100.00.

21T110M, 21", mahogany wood, tabletop, "Halolight," 1959, $100.00.

21T121, 21", metal, portable, 1959, $20.00.

21T208M, 21", mahogany wood, tabletop, "Halolight," 1959, $100.00.

21T305, 21", blond wood, tabletop, "Halolight," 1959, $110.00.

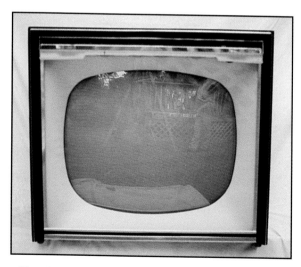

21T305M, 21", mahogany wood, tabletop, "Halolight," 1959, $100.00.

Black & White Television Sets

24C603, 21", blond wood, console, "Halolight," 1959, $110.00.

24T101, 24", wood, tabletop, 1957, $100.00.

24T301, 24", wood, tabletop, 1957, $100.00.

126B, 21", blond wood, console, chassis 1-510-1, "Halolight," 1952, $100.00.

120B, 21", blond wood, tabletop, chassis 1-510-1, "Halolight," 1952, $100.00.

120M, 21", mahogany wood, tabletop, chassis 1-510-1, "Halolight," 1952, $90.00.

126M, 21", mahogany wood, console, chassis 1-510-1, "Halolight," 1952, $90.00.

172K, 21", maple wood, console, double doors, chassis 1-508-3, "Halolight," 1952, $80.00.

172M, 21", mahogany wood, console, double doors, chassis 1-508-1, "Halolight," 1952, $80.00.

175B, 21", blond wood, tabletop, chassis 1-508-1, "Halolight," 1952, $80.00.

175M, 21", mahogany wood, tabletop, chassis 1-508-1, "Halolight," 1952, $75.00.

176B, 21", blond wood, console, chassis 1-508-3, "Halolight," 1952, $70.00.

1110X, 16", walnut wood, round tube, tabletop, chassis 1-329, 1950, $35.00.

1210X, 16", walnut wood, round tube, tabletop, chassis 1-381, 1950, $30.00.

2130B, 20", blond wood, round tube, console, chassis 1-462, 1951, $50.00.

2130M, 20", mahogany wood, round tube, console, chassis 1-462, 1951, $45.00.

2130W, 20", walnut wood, console, chassis 1-462, 1951, $45.00.

2140B, 20", blond wood, round tube, console, double doors, chassis 1-462, 1951, $45.00.

2140M, 20", mahogany wood, console, double doors, chassis 1-462, 1951, $40.00.

4120M, 14", mahogany wood, tabletop, chassis 1-260, 1951, $25.00.

4130B, 14", blond wood, console, chassis 1-260, 1951, $35.00.

4130E, 14", black lacquer wood, console, chassis 1-260, 1951, $40.00.

4130M, 14", mahogany wood, console, chassis 1-260, 1951, $30.00.

4130W, 14", walnut wood, console, chassis 1-260, 1951, $30.00.

5130B, 19", blond, round tube, console, chassis 1-290, 1950, $50.00.

5130M, 19", mahogany wood, round tube, console, chassis 1-290, 1950, $45.00.

5130W, 19", walnut wood, round tube, console, chassis 1-290, 1950, $45.00.

Symphonic

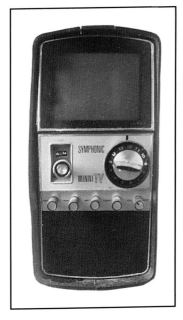

TPS-30, 3", white plastic, transistor, portable, AC-DC, 1968, $70.00.

TPS-5050, 3", black plastic, transistor, portable, AC-DC, 1968, $70.00.

Tele-King

C-816, 16", wood, console, 1949, $35.00.

KC-42, 24", wood, console, 1953, $15.00.

KD-42, 24", wood, console, double doors, 1953, $15.00.

KD-43, 24", wood, console, double doors, 1953, $15.00.

KD-71X, 17", wood, TV-radio/phono, console, 1952, $20.00.

T-510, 10", wood, tabletop, 1949, $90.00.

T-616, 16", wood, tabletop, 1949, $60.00.

T-712, 12", wood, tabletop, 1949, $65.00.

210, 10", wood, tabletop, 1948, $135.00.

310, 10", wood, console, 1948, $65.00.

410, 10", wood, tabletop, 1949, $95.00.

512, 12", wood, tabletop, 1949, $75.00.

612, 12", wood, console, 1949, $65.00.

710, 10", wood, console, 1949, $70.00.

Black & White Television Sets
Tele-Tone

TV-31, 14", mahogany wood, tabletop, rectangular CRT, 1950, $30.00.

TV-149, 7", wood, tabletop, 1948, $100.00.

TV-208TR, 7", cloth covered, portable, 1948, $85.00.

TV-209, 10", wood, tabletop, 1949, $80.00.

TV-220, 7", cloth-covered, portable, handle on top, 1949, $120.00.

TV-249, 10", wood, tabletop, 1949, $85.00.

TV-250, 10", Bakelite, tabletop, 1949, $90.00.

TV-254, 10", Bakelite, tabletop, 1949, $90.00.

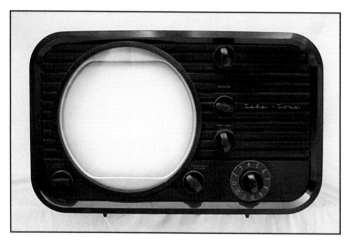

TV-255, 10", Bakelite, tabletop, 1949, $90.00.

TV-256, 10", Bakelite, tabletop, 1949, $90.00.

TV-279, 10", wood, console, 1949, $100.00.

TV-282, 10", wood, console, double doors, 1948, $80.00.

TV-285, 16", wood, tabletop, 1950, $35.00.

TV-286, 16", wood, console, 1950, $50.00.

TV-287, 12", wood, tabletop, 1950, $55.00.

Black & White Television Sets

TV-300, 10", black Bakelite, tabletop, 1950, $100.00.

TV-301, 10", brown Bakelite, tabletop, 1950, $100.00.

TV-305, 12", wood, tabletop, 1950, $65.00.

TV-306, 12", wood, tabletop, 1950, $40.00.

TV-307, 16", wood, console, 1950, $40.00.

TV-308, 19", wood, console, 1950, $25.00.

TV-315, 12", wood, tabletop, 1950, $40.00.

TV-318, 14", wood, tabletop, 1950, $35.00.

TV-322, 10", Bakelite, tabletop, 1950, $70.00.

TV-323, 10", Bakelite, tabletop, 1950, $70.00.

TV-324, 16", wood, tabletop, 1950, $20.00.

TV-337, 16", wood, tabletop, 1950, $20.00.

Tel-vision Labs Inc.

TR-7-1, 7", wood, kit TV, tabletop, chassis #TR10C-1, 1948, $180.00.

TR-10-1, 10", wood, kit TV, tabletop, chassis #TR10C-1, 1948, $150.00.

Television Assembly Co. (Snaider)

Auditorium, wood, projection, console, 1949, $75.00.

Champion, 12", wood, tabletop, 1949, $85.00.

Sports-View, 15", wood, tabletop 1949, $75.00.

P-520, projection, custom cabinet, 1949, $50.00.

Templetone Mfg. Co.

TV-1776, 7", wood, tabletop, with built-in magnifier, 1948, $500.00.

TMK Inc.

717, 1½", transistor, TV-radio, 1984, $45.00.

Black & White Television Sets

Transvision

KIT, 7", chassis and front panel, three channel tuner, 1947, $240.00, with factory built cabinet $320.00.

7BL, 7", wood, tabletop, five channel tuner, built-in magnifier, $375.00.

7CL, 7", wood, tabletop, 1947, $275.00.

7FL, 7", wood, tabletop, 1947, $275.00.

10A, 10", kit TV, with wood cabinet, 13 channel tuner, 1947, $175.00.

10BL, 10", wood, tabletop, with built-in magnifier, 1947, $225.00.

10CL, 10", wood, tabletop, with built-in magnifier, 1947, $225.00.

12BL, 12", wood, tabletop, 1947, $160.00.

Trans-Vue

90X, 12", mahogany wood, tabletop, 13 channel tuner, 1948, $90.00.

90XFM, 12", mahogany wood, TV-radio, tabletop, 13 channel tuner, 1948, $100.00.

90XFMB, 12", blond wood, TV-radio, tabletop, 13 channel, tuner, 1948, $120.00.

400, 12", blond wood, console, 12 channel tuner, 1949, $70.00.

601, 16", blond wood, console, 1949, $50.00.

610, 16", mahogany wood, console, 1949, $45.00.

Trad Television

13, projection, no cabinet, 1948, $60.00.

14, projection, no cabinet, 1948, $60.00.

Truetone (Western Auto Supply)

2985, 7", wood, tabletop, Raytheon 7DX21 chassis, 1949, $125.00.

D1090, 16", mahogany wood, console, 1949, $45.00.

D1990, 10", wood, tabletop, 1949, $65.00.

D1991, 10", wood, console, 1949, $50.00.

D1993, 10", wood, console, 1949, $50.00.

Black & White Television Sets

D1994, 10", mahogany, TV-radio/phono, console, double doors, 1949, $35.00.

D1996, 10", mahogany wood, console, 1949, $55.00.

D1997A, 10", mahogany wood, console, 1949, $75.00.

D1998A, 12", mahogany wood, console, 1949, $50.00.

D2044, 10", mahogany wood, tabletop, 1949, $45.00.

D2050A, 10", mahogany wood, tabletop, 1949, $65.00.

D2983, 10", mahogany wood, tabletop, 1949, $80.00.

Unisonic

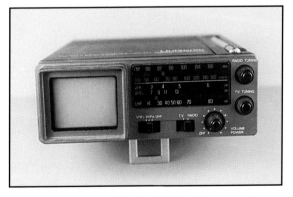

XL-990, 2", gray plastic, TV/radio, transistor, 1989, $45.00.

UST (United States Television)

UST (United States Television)

KRV-12831, 12", wood, TV-radio/phono, console, 1948, $50.00.

KRV-15831, 15", wood, TV-radio/phono, console, 1948, $40.00.

P-520, projection, rack mount system, 1949, $25.00.

T-502, 10", wood, TV-radio/phono, console, double doors, 1949, $45.00.

T-507, wood, projection, TV-radio/phono, console, 1949, $100.00.

T-508, leatherette covered, projection, TV-radio/phono, console, 1949, $100.00.

T-525, wood, projection, console, 1949, $120.00.

T530, wood, projection, console, 1949, $120.00.

T-10823, 10", wood, tabletop, 1949, $15.00.

T-15823, 15", wood, tabletop, 1949, $125.00.

621, wood, projection, console, 1949, $120.00.

Vidcraft Television Corp.

A-101, 10", metal, tabletop, video monitor, "Add-a-Vision," 1949, $75.00.

5700R, projection, chassis only, 1949, $40.00.

Black & White Television Sets

Videodyne

10FM, 10", wood, tabletop, 1948, $175.00.

10TV, 10", wood, tabletop, 13 channel tuner, 1948, $175.00.

12FM, 12", wood, tabletop, 1948, $150.00.

12TV, 12", wood, tabletop, 13 channel tuner, 1948, $150.00.

Viewtone

VP-100, 7", wood, tabletop, six channel tuner, "Futura," 1946, $450.00.

VP-101, 7", wood, TV-radio, console, six channel tuner, "Adventurer," 1946, $450.00.

VP-102, 7", wood, TV-radio/phono, console, 1946, $400.00.

Western Auto Supply (see Truetone)

Westinghouse

H-181, 10", wood, console, double doors, 1949, $85.00.

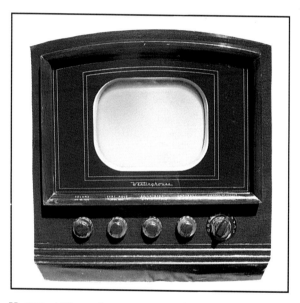

H-196, 10", mahogany wood, tabletop, 1949, $135.00.

H-207, 10", wood, TV-radio/phono, console, 1949, $70.00.

H216M, 16", mahogany wood, console, screen lifts up and forward, 1949, $175.00.

H-217, 12", wood, TV-radio/phono, console, 1949, $45.00.

Black & White Television Sets

H-223, 10", mahogany wood, tabletop, 1949, $85.00.

H-225, 12", wood, console, double doors, 1949, $55.00.

H-226, 12", wood, console, double doors, 1949, $55.00.

H231, 10", blond wood, TV-radio/phono, console, 1949, $55.00.

H-242, 12", wood, tabletop, 1948, $75.00.

H-251, 12", wood, tabletop, 1948, $75.00.

H-600T16, 16", wood, tabletop, 1948, $50.00.

H-601K12, 12", wood, console, 1948, $55.00.

H-602K12, 12", wood, console, 1948, $55.00.

H-603C12, 12", walnut wood, TV-radio/phono, console, 1948, $40.00.

H-604T10, 10", wood, tabletop, 1948, $85.00.

H-605T12, 12", wood, tabletop, 1948, $75.00.

Black & White Television Sets

H-608K10, 10", wood, console, 1948, $65.00.

H-610T10, 10", wood, tabletop, 1948, $75.00.

H-611C12, 12", wood, console, double doors, 1948, $60.00.

H-626T16, 16", wood, tabletop, 1950, $45.00.

H-627K16, 16", wood, console, 1950, $35.00.

H-628K16, 16", wood, console, 1950, $35.00.

H-629K16, 16", wood, console, 1950, $35.00.

H-637T14, 14", mahogany wood, tabletop, 1950, $35.00.

H-655, 17", wood, console, 1951, $35.00.

H-657, 17", wood, console, 1951, $35.00.

H-738, 17", wood, tabletop, 1951, $25.00.

H-739, 17", wood, tabletop, 1951, $25.00.

H-760, 21", wood, tabletop, 1951, $15.00.

H761, 21", wood, tabletop, 1951, $15.00.

660C17, 17", wood, TV-radio/phono, console, 1951, $20.00.

Zenith

A1512J, 16", metal, portable, 1956, $35.00.

G2322, 12", Bakelite, tabletop, chassis 23G22, "Claridge," 1950, $95.00.

G2322R, 12", mahogany wood, tabletop, chassis 23G22, "Claridge," 1950, $150.00.

G2322RZ, 12", mahogany wood, tabletop, chassis 23G24, "Claridge," 1949, $150.00.

Black & White Television Sets

G2327, 12", walnut wood, tabletop, chassis 23G24, "Garfield," 1950, $150.00.

G2327E, 12", white lacquer wood, tabletop, chassis 23G24, "Eskimo," 1950, $165.00.

G2327R7, 12", leatherette covered wood, tabletop, chassis 23G24, 1950, $125.00.

G2340R, 12", mahogany wood, console, chassis 23G22, "Saratoga," 1950, $100.00.

G2340RZ, 12", mahogany wood, console, chassis 23G24, "Saratoga," 1950, $100.00.

G2340Z, 12", walnut wood, console, chassis 23G24, "Ensign," 1950, $100.00.

G2350RZ, 12", mahogany wood, console, chassis 23G24, "Adams," 1950, $110.00.

G2353E, 12", blond wood, console, chassis 23G22, "Biltmore," 1950, $125.00.

G2353RZ1, 12", mahogany wood, console, chassis 23G24Z1, "Harrison," 1950, $110.00.

G2355EZ, 12", blond wood, console, chassis 23G24, "Tyler," 1950, $110.00.

G2356R, 12", mahogany wood, console, double doors, chassis 23G24, "Harrison," 1950, $110.00.

G2420E, 12", blond wood, tabletop, chassis 24G20, "Wilshire," 1950, $170.00.

G2420R, 12", mahogany wood, tabletop, chassis 24G20, "Newport," 1950, $150.00.

Black & White Television Sets

G2437EZ1, 16", blond wood, console, double doors, chassis 24G26Z1, "Filmore," 1950, $110.00.

G2437RZ, 16", mahogany wood, console, double doors, chassis 24G26, "Jackson," 1950, $100.00.

G2438RZ, 16", mahogany wood, console, chassis 24G26, "Lincoln," 1950, $90.00.

G2439RZ, 16", mahogany wood, console, double doors, chassis 24G26, "Monroe," 1950, $90.00.

G2441, 16", walnut wood, console, chassis 24G22, "Endow," 1950, $100.00.

G2441R, 16", mahogany wood, console, chassis 24G24, "Lexington," 1950, $90.00.

G2442E, 16", blond wood, console, chassis 24G22, "Waldorf," 1950, $110.00.

G2442R, 16", mahogany wood, console, chassis 24G24, "Mayfair," 1950, $90.00.

G2448R, 16", mahogany wood, console, chassis 24G24, "Warwick," 1950, $90.00.

G2448Z, 16", walnut wood, console, chassis 24G26, "Warwick," 1950, $90.00.

G2845R, 12", mahogany wood, console, 28G20, 1948, $110.00.

G2951, 16", walnut wood, console, chassis 29G20, "Stratosphere," 1949, $120.00.

G2951R, 16", mahogany wood, console, chassis 29G20, "Stratosphere," 1949, $120.00.

G2952R, 16", mahogany wood, console, chassis 29G20, "St. Regis," 1949, $120.00.

G2957, 12", walnut wood, TV-radio/phono, console, double doors, chassis 23G22, "Endue," 1950, $75.00.

G2957R, 12", mahogany wood, TV-radio/phono, console, double doors, chassis 23G22, "Riviera," 1950, $75.00.

G2958R, 12", mahogany wood, TV-radio/phono, console, double doors, chassis 23G22, "Regent," 1950, $75.00.

G3059R, 16", mahogany wood, TV-radio/phono, console, chassis 24G24, "Sheraton," 1950, $75.00.

Black & White Television Sets

G3062, 16", walnut wood, TV-radio/phono, console, chassis 24G23, "Classic," 1950, $70.00.

G3173RZ, 16", mahogany wood, TV-radio/phono, console, chassis 23G24, "Madison," 1950, $65.00.

G3275RZ, 16", mahogany wood, TV-radio/phono, console, chassis 24G26, "Washington," 1950, $65.00.

H2029, 17", wood, tabletop, chassis 20H20, "Marlowe," 1951, $35.00.

H2030, 17", wood, tabletop, chassis 20H20, "Hardy," 1951, $35.00.

H2226R, 12", mahogany wood, tabletop, chassis 22H20, "Wharton," 1951, $80.00.

H2227E, 12", blond wood, tabletop, chassis 22H20, "Walpole," 1951, $80.00.

H2229R, 17", mahogany wood, tabletop, chassis 22H22, "Hardy," 1951, $35.00.

H2253E, 17", blond wood, tabletop, chassis 22H21, "Goldsmith," 1951, $35.00.

H2330R, 17", mahogany wood, tabletop, 1951, chassis 23H22, "Blake," 1951, $35.00.

H2437E, 16", blond wood, console, chassis 24H20, "Fielding," 1951, $80.00.

H2438R, 16", mahogany, wood, console, chassis 24H20, "Aldrich," 1951, $80.00.

H2445R, 19", mahogany wood, console, chassis 24H21, "Teninson," 1951, $130.00.

H2447R, 19", mahogany wood, console, chassis 24H21, "Byron," 1951, $130.00.

H3267R, 16", mahogany wood, TV-radio/phono, console, chassis 24H20, "Hawthorne," 1951, $60.00.

H3477R, 19", mahogany wood, TV-radio/phono, console, chassis 24H21, "Thackeray," 1951, $65.00.

H3469E, 16", blond wood, TV-radio/phono, console, chassis 24H20, "Wordsworth," 1951, $80.00.

K1812, 17", Bakelite, tabletop, chassis 19K20, "Tudor," 1951, $35.00.

K1815E, 17", blond wood, tabletop, chassis 19K20, 1951, $35.00.

K1820, 17", Bakelite, tabletop, "Norfolk," 1952, $25.00.

K1846R, 17", mahogany wood, console, chassis 19K20, "Stafford," 1952, $25.00.

K1880R, 17", mahogany wood, TV-radio/phono, console, chassis 19K20, "Sutherland," 1952, $20.00.

K2230E, 21", blond wood, tabletop, chassis 21K20, 1953, $25.00.

K2230R, 21", wood, tabletop, chassis 21K20, "Inverness," 1952, $20.00.

K2260R, 21", mahogany wood, console, chassis 21K20, "Malborough," 1952, $25.00.

Black & White Television Sets

L2894H, 27", wood, TV-radio/phono, console, 1953, $100.00.

T1814, 17", metal, tabletop, chassis 16T20, 1955, $45.00.

T1816, 17", metal, tabletop, chassis 16T20, 1955, $45.00.

T2250, 21", wood, console, chassis 19R21, 1955, $25.00.

T2294, 27 ", wood, TV-radio/phono, console, 1955, $25.00.

T2360, 21", wood, console, chassis 19R21, 1955, $25.00.

27T965R, 12", mahogany, console, chassis 27F20, "Broadmoor," 1948, $120.00.

28T925E, 10", blond wood, tabletop, chassis 28F20, "Biltmore," 1948, $200.00.

28T925R, 10", mahogany wood, tabletop, chassis 28F20, "Mayflower," 1949, $180.00.

28T926E, 12", blond wood, tabletop, chassis 28F25, "Saratoga," 1949, $175.00.

28T926R, 12", mahogany wood, tabletop, chassis 28F25, "Claridge," 1949, $160.00.

28T960E, 12", blond wood, console, chassis 28F20, "Waldorf," 1949, $140.00.

28T960K, 12", Cordovan wood, console, chassis 28F20, "Derby," 1949, $100.00.

28T961E, 10", blond wood, console, chassis 28F21, "Wilshire," 1949, $150.00.

28T962R, 12", mahogany wood, console, chassis 28F20, "Warwick," 1949, $125.00.

28T963, 10", walnut wood, console, chassis 28F21, "Newport," 1949, $130.00.

28T964R, 16", mahogany wood, console, chassis 28F23, "Stratosphere," 1948, $130.00.

37T996RLP, 16", mahogany wood, TV-radio/phono, console, chassis 28F23, "Sovereign," 1948, $80.00.

37T998RLP, 12", mahogany wood, TV-radio/phono, console, chassis 28F20, "Gotham," 1948, $90.00.

42T999RLP, 16", wood, TV-radio/phono, console, chassis 28F23, "Marlborough," 1948, $80.00.

"...BROUGHT TO YOU IN LIVING COLOR"

Do you remember watching color television for the first time?

It was a Sunday in January 1969 when my family bought their first color television. I sat down that night with a bowl of popcorn and watched "The Wonderful World of Disney" in color for the very first time! It was a luxury to have a color television in those days.

Color television was part of the pioneers' dreams from the very beginning. As early as the twenties, the discussion of color television development was well under way. It was dismissed as being an immediate goal, which was the logical thing to do considering the hurdles still to overcome with black and white television.

As World War II came to a close, efforts resumed in a serious manner towards color television development. Although there was much more development to come for black and white television, there now was a definite working scheme to reproduce those pictures faithfully. Color television needed a scheme on how to be reproduced, as well as how the transmission of those signals was to occur. It became a technical obstacle, and a legal point of contention, on whether the color signal would be compatible with the existing black and white signal. Engineering demands in the post-war era were strained. The rising demands of better goods in large quantities only confounded the engineers further. With these and many other obstacles, it was unfortunate that color television technology did not evolve as fast as black and white.

The battle for color finally emerged between two giants the television industry, RCA (Radio Corporation of America) and CBS (Colombia Broadcast System). At the time, RCA, the larger giant, was reasonably confident that their color system would reign because it was widely accepted by the technical leaders of that era as being the clear choice. RCA often had their way before, but by an unusual line of logic reasoned by the FCC (Federal Communications Commission) on October 11, 1950, CBS became the early winner.

The CBS color system was largely mechanical. The system consisted of a tri-color spinning wheel. Many technical experts realized that this system would not be practical. The size of the color wheel to obtain a 19" picture screen was around three feet in diameter. The cabinet to house this color wheel setup would have to be very large.

Also, anything mechanical is prone to wear, and there is noise generated by the movement of mechanical components. To the CBS systems credit, the picture was very good, as few collectors who have these early sets can attest. All of these problems could have been acceptable except for one, the CBS system operated on 405 scanning lines of information, the current black and white system operated on 525 scanning lines of information.

To the RCA color system credit, the system was fully electronic; it did not utilize any mechanical components to generate a color picture. This was a great advantage compared to the generated noise and space requirements of the CBS system. The biggest advantage was that the RCA color system was compatible with the existing black and white 525 scanning lines format. RCA published a petition paper to the FCC on January 21,1951, outlining the technical aspects, advantages, and compatibility of their color system. Shortly after the FCC received RCA's petition they reconsidered their decision and proclaimed the RCA color system the national standard.

The first electronic color televisions had 15" picture tubes. Most of the 15" tubes were used only in the first years of production. The popular 21" picture tube, used through the mid-1960s, were well under development the year that 15" color sets were introduced. The problem with the 21" tube was that they could not be produced in any large quantity. The first 21" picture tubes had a metal envelop, which was a popular way to manufacture large tubes in that era. It was difficult to produce a large picture tube with a completely glass envelope that was rugged and sturdy. Some early manufacturers such as Motorola and CBS used a 19" picture tube. These 19" tubes were used only for two years and were often replaced with the later 21" tubes. CBS and Motorola made picture tube replacement kits to convert the 19" picture tube to the popular 21" picture tube.

COLOR TELEVISION SETS

Arvin

15-550, 15", walnut wood, console, 1954, $650.00.

CBS-Colombia

RX89, 15", blond wood, prototype, console, 1953, rare.

RX90, 15", mahogany wood, console, double doors, 1954, $700.00.

205C1, 19", mahogany wood, console, 1955, $375.00.

205C2, 19", mahogany, wood, console, double doors, 1955, $400.00.

General Electric

15CL100, 15", mahogany wood, console, 1954, $550.00.

Motorola

**16CK1, 15", walnut wood, console, chassis
TS-900, 1954, $750.00.**

19CK1, 19", walnut wood, console, chassis TS-902, 1954,
$600.00.

19CK1B, 19", blond wood, console, chassis TS-902, 1954,
$625.00.

19CT1, 19", walnut wood, console, chassis TS-902, 1954, $600.00.

19CT1B, 19", blond wood, console, chassis TS-902, 1954, $625.00.

21CK3B, 21", blond wood, console, chassis TS-905, 1957, $325.00.

21CK3M, 21", mahogany wood, console, chassis TS-905, 1957, $300.00.

21CT1, 21", walnut wood, console, chassis TS-904, 1955, $450.00.

21CT1B, 21", blond wood, console, chassis TS-904, 1955, $475.00.

21CT2, 21", walnut wood, console, chassis TS-905, 1956, $300.00.

21CT2B, 21", blond wood, console, chassis TS-905, 1956, $325.00.

21CT2BA, 21", blond wood, console, chassis WTS-905, 1957, $275.00.

21CT2M, 21", mahogany wood, console, chassis TS-905, 1956, $325.00.

21CT2MA, 21", mahogany wood, console, chassis WTS-905, 1957, $475.00.

RCA

CT100, 15", mahogany wood, console, 1954, $500.00.

21-CT-55, 21", mahogany wood, console, 1955, $300.00.

21-CT-600, 21", mahogany wood, console, 1955, $300.00.

21-CT-66-2U, 21", mahogany wood, console, chassis CTC-4, 1956, $175.00.

21-CT-66-3U, 21", birch wood, console, double doors, chassis CTC-4, 1956, $175.00.

21-CT-7857, 21",
blond wood,
console, chas-
sis CTC-5, 1956,
$160.00.

21-CT-837, 21", blond metal cabinet, console, chassis CTC-9,
1957, $100.00.

Color Television Sets

Sentinel

816C, 21", mahogany wood, console, 1956, $275.00.

Sparton

16A211, 15", mahogany wood, console, 1955, $625.00.

Stromberg-Carlson

K-1, 15", walnut wood, console, 1955, $450.00.

Westinghouse

H840CK15, 15", mahogany wood, console, double doors, 1954, $600.00.

Zenith

Prototype, 15", oak wood, console, 1953, rare.

ABOUT THE AUTHORS

Bryan Durbal and Glenn Bubenheimer are members of the Michigan Antique Radio Club, and can be found at many of the radio collector swap meets throughout the Midwest. Both are known for their collection interest in early television and radios. Their combined collection contains over 300 post-war televisions. Bryan operates a small business and an on-line vintage television museum called Channel One Vintage Television in which he displays, buys, and sells vintage televisions, radios, and related items. Bryan's main television collection interest is small tabletop sets from the late 1940s. Glenn's collecting hobbies are not only focused on vintage televisions, but also include early television advertising material and memorabilia, early video tape machines, antique radios, and telephones. Glenn also has interest in odd brand name and one-of-a-kind black and white televisions and a strong interest early production color televisions and has many rare examples of these technological wonders. With the increasing popularity of vintage television collection, Bryan and Glenn are always hunting for new television items to add to their ever-expanding television collection.

Channel One Vintage Television
718 East Grandriver
Fowlerville, Michigan 48836
Visit us on the web at: http://members.aol.com/channel1tv
E-mail at: channel1tv@aol.com

Authors Bryan Durbal (left) and Glenn Bubenheimer (right).

Schroeder's
ANTIQUES
Price Guide
. . . is the #1 best-selling
antiques & collectibles value guide on the market today,
and here's why . . .

8½ x 11 • 612 Pgs. • PB • $12.95

• *More than 300 advisors, well-known dealers, and top-notch collectors work together with our editors to bring you accurate information regarding pricing and identification.*

• *More than 45,000 items in almost 500 categories are listed along with hundreds of sharp original photos that illustrate not only the rare and unusual, but the common, popular collectibles as well.*

• *Each large close-up shot shows important details clearly. Every subject is represented with histories and background information, a feature not found in any of our competitors' publications.*

• *Our editors keep abreast of newly developing trends, often adding several new categories a year as the need arises.*

If it merits the interest of today's collector, you'll find it in *Schroeder's*. And you can feel confident that the information we publish is up to date and accurate. Our advisors thoroughly check each category to spot inconsistencies, listings that may not be entirely reflective of market dealings, and lines too vague to be of merit. Only the best of the lot remains for publication.

Without doubt, you'll find
**SCHROEDER'S ANTIQUES
PRICE GUIDE**
the only one to buy for
reliable information and values.

COLLECTOR BOOKS
A Division of Schroeder Publishing Co., Inc.